LORAN INC.

Conseillers à la direction d'entreprises

2050 RUE MANSFIELD
BUREAU 1404
MONTRÉAL (QUÉBEC)
H3A 1Y9

Bank Marketing For The 90s

4.7.9

Bank Marketing For The 90s

New Ideas From 55 Of The Best Marketers In Banking

Don Wright

John Wiley & Sons, Inc.

New York · Chichester · Brisbane · Toronto · Singapore

Copyright © 1991 by John Wiley & Sons, Inc.

All rights reserved. Published simultaneously in Canada.

Reproduction or translation of any part of this work beyond that permitted by Section 107 or 108 of the 1976 United States Copyright Act without the permission of the copyright owner is unlawful. Requests for permission or further information should be addressed to the Permissions Department, John Wiley & Sons, Inc.

This publication is designed to provide accurate and authoritative information in regard to the subject matter covered. It is sold with the understanding that the publisher is not engaged in rendering legal, accounting, or other professional service. If legal advice or other expert assistance is required, the services of a competent professional person should be sought. *From a Declaration of Principles jointly adopted by a Committee of the American Bar Association and a Committee of Publishers.*

Library of Congress Cataloging in Publication Data

Wright, Don, 1915–
    Bank marketing for the 90s: new ideas from 55 of the best marketers in banking / Don Wright.
      p. cm.
    Includes index.
    ISBN 0-471-52264-3
    1. Bank marketing.   I. Title.
HG1616.M3W75 1991
332.1′0688—dc20   90-25683
                                             CIP

Printed in the United States of America

91 92 10 9 8 7 6 5 4 3 2 1

To Our In-Law Children

Roberta Wright
Larry Minnix
Amram Shapiro

Contents

Introduction

T his book contains the best marketing ideas for financial institutions in the 1990s, as produced, used, and proved by the most respected marketers in the banking industry.

In putting this book together, I called the State Bankers' Associations and asked for the names of the best bank marketers in each of their states. Many named chief executives at leading banks; some named marketing officers or other senior executives. I asked each of the executives for their best marketing idea and requested permission to use it in this book. These banks ranged in size from $20 million in assets to well over $20 billion. Their communities are equally diverse and representative. Some gave me more than one idea, and many of these thoughts were so valuable that they are also included in this publication.

Deep and encouraging changes have occurred in the place and influence of marketing in banks, in how it is organized and carried out, and the results expected. In writing my book, *The Effective Bank Director*, six years ago, I also asked bankers for their best marketing ideas. They related to advertising and promotion and were considered mainly the responsibility of marketing departments. Now, bankers are talking much more about the marketing role in hiring, training, and organizing. There is a new recognition that many banks are primarily staffed with employees and supervisors who, as one chief executive put it, are "centered on systems and accounting." While we always must have some people high in systems and accounting ability, years ago the industry discouraged people who were more people- or idea-oriented. This created an imbalance in lending and management which goes to the heart of performance, not only in marketing, but within the whole institution.

We naturally have on our boards and in many senior management positions those who would describe themselves as "bottom-line people." They want results—preferably today. Those two groups—systems people and bottom-line people—were the dominant forces in the financial industry in its regulated, protected years, and they were usually successful. But the exceptions, like A. P. Giannini, J. P. Morgan, and, in Dallas, Bob Thornton, built institutions and pioneered new fields. Not all of the pioneers became famous. Many simply broke new ground, and not always successfully; but they kept banking from being contained behind gates and barred tellers' cages. It is encouraging that many banks now are radically changing their hiring practices by adding more employees with people skills and, even occasionally, creative thinkers with longer range views. The head of the School of Banking at Southern Methodist University says that when Citicorp and other banks come to the campus to recruit, they no longer require an accounting major; they now say, "Give me your best student." A broad educational background will better serve the students when they move up in the organization and face a complicated world of fast-paced change.

A word frequently used by good marketers is *training*. Some banks today spend what would once have been considered outrageous amounts of money and time on training, and they do not cut the training budget with every dip in profits. "Marketing people" are less separated from the "real bankers." Those who are considered important in the marketing effort are much more involved in the whole training program, frequently having taken this over from personnel or human resources. They are often deeply involved in designing and pricing bank services.

In the last six to eight years, there has also been a major move away from the style of organization in which all the operating people, who represent the largest percentage of the employees with extensive customer contact, report to a systems- and detail-oriented cashier or other supervisor. Now more of the departments important to sales and public image report to marketing-oriented people who must also be sound, all-around bankers. They must know not just marketing, but how their areas of responsibility should serve the customer and protect the bank.

Compared to a half-dozen years ago, I have also found an increased emphasis on information about customers which, coupled with employee judgment, enables a bank to confidently sell services that fit the needs and wants of the customers. A financial institution can have a big advantage here. When we sell a product, we generally create a customer who can be retained and easily persuaded to buy many more services. Some financial institutions are even able to keep customers wherever they are in the world, even hundreds or thousands of miles away. This is done with the help of information that can be called up quickly to answer the customer's need. One knowledgable banker told me, "We must convince our customer that this is a place to bank, not just for now but for the rest of your life." This customer information also helps the banker recognize who is a prospect and for what. That is half-way to making a sale.

I believe the most important realization of the last half-dozen years is that marketing is the very foundation of our business and is necessary for its survival. It determines what kind and quality of business the organization gets. Hence, good banking institutions have raised their marketing activities to the chief executive officer level.

However, very few of the bankers I met felt that they have instilled a marketing orientation and attitude all the way down in the organization. They are right. Many bank employees have never "signed on" for this. Others pretend an

interest they do not feel and are not really looking at their bank or their jobs any differently
than before. They do not recognize, as one
banker said, that "everyone has a customer."
They are the dinosaurs of the business. Getting
real marketing ability and commitment all the
way down, and at the same time maintaining
high standards of quality, calls for a long and
costly effort. It requires change in attitude, as
well as in skills. But it is immensely worthwhile.

The best marketers recognize that getting and
keeping business is the foremost part of the job
of the CEO. Market position and share are on
the same general level of importance as staff
and management development, earnings, capital, and liquidity in evaluating management performance. The satisfied customer is the best
source of business. Getting business by buying
banks or savings and loans, or paying more for
certificates in certain markets, is often appro-
priate. However, the satisfied customer is the
core of the business world. Marketing efforts
which build on this core business focus on getting and keeping satisfied customers. The whole
team must be committed to this, and the CEO
and staff must have it near the top of the
agenda. All this is impossible unless the CEO
is really committed, as most of the CEOs of
good banks are.

I spent 38 years in banking. As a CEO for 21
years, I had to focus on all industry aspects,
including asset quality and profits. It is now
a pleasure to see that, as one banker put it,
"Marketing has become the way we live our
daily lives." I feel much more confident of the
future of our industry than I did before writing
this book.

The good marketing executives are not hot-shots. They are sound bankers who make money through overall good management. Marketing is only one aspect of this good management—but a crucial one.

PART ONE

The New World
Of Banking

Good bank managers are recognizing what other businesses, including "mom and pop" stores, have always known: Successful selling and quality service are the only ways to create and maintain a business. Any organization must sell enough good business to keep its doors open and remain profitable.

In the past few years, competition from all kinds of institutions, both near and far, has intensified in an environment of more rapid economic change, improved technology, and an increase in the number and complexity of banking services. Good bankers know that the best way to meet this competition is to hold on to good customers and add as many new ones as possible.

Good bankers also see marketing as a profit maker rather than a cost. Generally, marketing now costs less than the advertising and promotions of the past except as it emphasizes better training and achieves better service. Good service *does* cost more.

This is where training comes in. It does little good to change the title of the cashier to "cashier and sales representative." What must change is *attitude* and *ability*. This generally requires one-on-one training.

As a banker, I made a lot of sales calls and enjoyed them. But when I retired and started a new business, I learned to focus on *results*. I was spending a lot of money on marketing which could not continue without profitable sales.

Marketing as described by Len Huck, retired CEO of Valley National Bank and Valley National Corporation of Arizona, focuses on selling profitable products. He adds, "Marketing now has the attention of top management. . . . This is where we always wanted it to be, but we don't have it all the way down." In making calls to outstanding marketers, I encountered few who believed they had developed a true "marketing culture." Why is this so hard and costly to develop? Why does its establishment often cause so much turnover in the bank as a whole? In general, it does not fit with the kind of people we have hired, the way we have been organized, and the pattern of our past thinking.

It is easy for distant managers to think that their employees are marketing when actually they are merely saying the right words, keeping a low profile, and, perhaps, camouflaging the loss of real customer activity by larger transactions. For instance, many banks today do not have as many customers as they had three years ago, although their total footings may be larger.

One of the toughest questions for management is how to get a non-figure fact into a computer printout. One good, but typically operations-oriented, department head said, "I am judged by the cost and efficiency of my department as measured by the computer, and there is nothing in there about customer satisfaction."

In the future, banks will have more "people" people. Operating areas will report to marketing-oriented bankers. But those bankers must know their stuff—and not just about marketing.

All the old feuds between operations- and marketing-centered activities must be eliminated. So must the new feuds between lenders and loan closers, bank managers and operations centers, and branch officers and company headquarters. The chairman of one bank with a deep commitment to a sales culture regularly tells employees in the operations center, "We can not perform for our customers any better than your work permits us to." The same message needs to go to credit departments, new accounts departments, trust departments, and every section of the bank, whether it has direct or indirect contact with the public. In today's competitive era, where dollars spent must go farther, those who think that marketing is not necessary may soon be looking for another job.

There has been increasing creativity in marketing strategies within the banking industry— in the widespread use of supermarket banks, lending by telephone, telemarketing, packaging services—making marketing dollars do double duty and placing emphasis on marketing supported with technology. In one bank holding company, senior executives work a few days every year in individual banks to see how their products are being received and what is needed that is new and different. New and creative concepts, which in the past seemed "un-bankerlike," are working effectively in many fine institutions.

Unfortunately, even in some of the most prestigious institutions, a high percentage of what goes on is without regard for the fact that there *is* a customer who uses the end product. A poll done by the Bank Marketing Association shows that bankers rate our industry next to the bottom in sophistication of marketing technology. Within the industry, though, great emphasis among the best marketers is placed on backing marketing with technology that provides real information and is speedily obtainable. This information may include what services the customers are using and what their needs are. This information must not just be in the computer—it must be known and used by people in the bank.

Some institutions are way ahead of others in using technology. As banks are freed to offer a wide range of other services (as some kinds of financial institutions are already doing), the bank with full, reliable, and up-to-date knowledge of the customer has a big lead.

During the early 1980s, in Texas, many banks forgot what one banker called "blocking and tackling" in their eagerness to create a "go-go" image. Most of those bankers have in truth gone.

The fact that there are so many advances in marketing does not mean the old concepts are all dead. Soundness, strength, integrity, community participation, and service have been at the core of good banking in this country for more than 150 years and are still the centerpiece of selling the bank and its services. Unless customers perceive that the bank is sound and well run, no amount or kind of marketing will succeed for long. Good marketing still speaks to quality, to strength, and to history. It says to the customer in a believable way, "We will be here when you need us, in good times and bad."

Marketing For Survival And Progress

The legendary
Dallas banker,
Fred Florence,
said, "It is not we
who grow but our
customers, and it
is our job to help
them." What a
pleasant
assignment!

As a banker, I was welcomed everywhere. "Yes, I will be glad to have lunch with you," prospects responded. People readily answered my telephone calls. I was not left to cool my heels in the waiting room. Bankers, including assistant vice presidents and tellers, have a big advantage over other salespeople. As a banker, I had directors, officers, employees (and a marketing budget) to help me. When customers entered the door, they provided invaluable information about new banking needs.

How different it was when I started my new company. People—bankers—often did not return my calls. I had no staff, no employees, and not even one customer. Marketing was not a part of my focus, but all of it. I constantly asked, "What can I sell and to whom?"

Every time I developed a service in this new business it had to sell another service. Every time I sold a client, this sale needed to lead to another client. Otherwise, I could not afford enough marketing to be successful. Even so, selling was a major cost. When I lost money, the only way to break even and stay in business was to sell more.

I was right where most businesses have always been. These ideas were known by commercial banks in the old days of enclosed tellers cages and loan platforms. Later, many got big and sophisticated, created marketing budgets, and often made marketing the responsibility of a separate department, with a budget to be cut if profits fell. When selling ceased to be a part of the everyday job of everyone from the CEO down, marketing became a stepchild, a sideshow, often looked down upon by the "real bankers."

Do not be too proud to be a sales professional. A banker today has little room for arrogance. We are part of an industry that has lost market share for decades and, generally, is not earning enough on assets. We need to be seeking more trust and acceptance and building for the future, not taking it for granted.

Today I am selling more services in my business. When I call bankers, I often get the sense on the telephone that the banker is thinking, "I wonder if you are really important enough for me to talk to." I do not resent that. Meeting that attitude is a part of selling. People whose positions are not "awe-inspiring" are often too important to talk to me. I do not resent that either. That is the life of most professional salespeople. However, about two hundred top marketing banking executives returned my calls. I never once sensed the "I am too big to talk to you" attitude, and I talked to some of banking's biggest. Good marketing begins with the open and businesslike attitude of the CEO and other top executives, and this will be apparent as soon as you walk in or even call someone in the bank on the telephone. It is also apparent to any new employee or officer that this is in the atmosphere.

Most of our bank employees and officers originally came into the industry because they had some skills and experience in jobs that needed to be filled. Generally, this involved figures or systems. Some had been examiners, accountants, auditors, or controller types. Banks recruited almost exclusively from colleges and those without heavy training in accounting need not have applied. Later, when these people were far up the ladder, we would suddenly say to them, "Now it is time for you to be a salesperson (or manager), and many went elsewhere.

Late in life I received a black belt in judo. Maybe it was for just hanging in there and getting old, but it meant a lot to me. I have never been athletic. The fact that the teacher, or *sensai*, simply took it for granted that I would succeed and taught me how to do it, made the award possible. I enjoyed the whole experience and especially getting acquainted with the different kinds of people who take judo, including the young Oriental men who voluntarily came out without pay to practice with me so I could pass the test.

When I first came into banking I posted the old Boston style general ledger with pen and ink. This job provided everything but the high stool, green eyeshades, and sleeve garters. The fact that I had no other job in sight with which to support a family of five forced me to go in every day and struggle with the most detailed kind of a job for which I was totally unsuited. But I was convinced that I could succeed in this business. This holds true on the other side as well. If we want to get technicians and systems people to pay attention to marketing, and even tolerate the change, they must be convinced that they can succeed and there is a better time ahead.

Selling Throughout The Banking Environment

People can adapt. Accounting is thought of as a very structured profession; however, one of the most creative men I know began his career as an accounting instructor. To encourage our employees to be more sales-oriented, it is important to reward them for recognizing the customer's financial needs and meeting them. They must know they can win. My office is near the investment department of our bank. It is a delight to see the monthly awarding of checks for cross-selling and hear the expressions of pleasure from the winners. For some it is recognition of a skill they did not know they had. Not only that, the cross-selling award is a windfall that may pay for a new refrigerator that will not fit into the already overloaded family budget.

Give the person you ask to enter the field of selling a chance to win and feel good, along with recognition and some kind of extra compensation. Venturing into selling (or any other new field) can be scary. Many banks make early targets easy to hit. Even doing passably well in a new field can be a confidence builder. It takes nerve and determination to make such a change. Those who have that are special.

I have already mentioned one business I started since retiring. Another I have expanded involves investing. That puts me in the position to talk to managers in other industries. Every CEO in these companies knows that if his product does not sell, sooner or later there will be a special meeting of the board to select his successor.

In most industries nothing happens without first focusing on the market.—I mean real market research to develop products that will sell. Engineering, product design, packaging, and transportation all are geared to getting, expanding, and keeping a share of a market.

Financial executives, like those in other industries, should be measuring the volume of real customer activity and the trends. We must look beyond this quarter. Shun window dressing actions that are costly and short term in nature.

Len Huck, retired Chief of Valley National in Arizona, who came up through marketing says, "Boards should be a great marketing source, but generally they are not." Why not? Directors efforts should be *organized*. Ask them to do things with which they are comfortable. This will vary from one director to another, but most are salespeople in their own businesses and would be in ours. But, as one Dallas director said, "They must feel that they count." One of the best ways to assure that is to involve them in planning.

Bank stockholders and stock analysts are similarly sensitive to the need and ability of the bank to market against the competition. The good financial marketers are using techniques that have been successful in other industries. We cannot build the bank to suit our personal tastes. It must be shaped to suit the market.

The response given by some banks and savings and loan associations to losing business has been to pay more for deposits and make bigger and riskier loans. This creates larger figures and conceals the loss of real customer activity. This self-deception is not so easy in other industries. For example, the proprietor of a cafeteria always knows the number of people going through the line and whether total sales are up or down. Bank executives must be able to make the same measurements. In most community banks, lobby traffic, number of accounts, loans made, accounts opened and closed, and the reasons for closing provide measures of the pulse of the bank. Real marketing involves doing a better job with our customers in our own market areas. It enables us to hold down the cost of money and, thus, make stronger and more profitable loans, as well as do more to satisfy and keep employees.

When I asked bankers for their best marketing ideas, almost no one mentioned their board of directors as a source of help. We cannot afford to miss that resource. One of the few remaining advantages bankers have over Merrill Lynch, and many others offering financial services, is the possibility of creating and using an effective local board of directors. I am not suggesting that directors should be chosen mainly for their ability to bring in business. But, as one young CEO of a $60 million bank said to me, "We cannot afford advertising that will compete with the big banks, nor can we have full-time marketers hitting the street. We must have help from our directors."

Have a system for your board to make referrals, act on them, and report results to the director. It is easy for directors to get two referrals a month. But if the lead is hot, the director should get it into the bank right away. He should know whom in the bank to call. The banker *must* follow up on director referrals or he will kill the director's interest.

Directors are a great potential resource because they know the *good* business. They can easily open doors and lend their influence. Organizations should create a system to develop director referrals. In one bank in which I served as a director, the CEO would pass out two forms at the end of each board meeting and say, "Please get us two referrals before the next meeting." After the meeting I would go out and fight my own battles, as did the other directors. Twenty-five days later a young lady from the bank would call to remind me of the board meeting and say, "And please bring your referrals." Oh, my goodness, I had forgotten about that!

But who is the new young doctor coming in to join the local clinic? I heard of someone planning a swimming pool; they might need financing. I know of a small company that is expanding; they may need a line of credit. Almost any active director can think of two referrals in five minutes. However, having an organized system provides greater assurance that these leads will be followed up.

When I give this talk at bank conventions, often some director comes up and says, "On the last several referrals I have given my bank, I heard nothing back. I ran into the prospect on the 19th hole and I was embarrassed because I did not know if the bank had called on him." The director has the impression that his suggestions are not thought worthwhile—and he is right.

One director whose business wrote about 300 checks a month to suppliers turned them over to look at the endorsement and to see where they were deposited. He realized that only a few of his customers were doing business with his bank. He wrote a letter to each supplier saying, "I would like you to listen to an officer from my bank." The bank sent a good salesperson, and reported that business was obtained in almost 100 percent of those cases. Of course, nobody is that good a salesperson. The salesperson succeeded many times due to the director's influence.

Suggest to directors ways to help that fit in with their business and personality. If the director has a plaque on his office wall showing he is a board member, it can be the basis of positive conversation about the bank.

A director in a "retreat" pledged to make one quality call a month. This is a very valuable commitment. The most powerful business-getting approach for any financial institution is for director and banker to sit across the desk from the prospect in his office and say, "We sure would like to have you for a customer." The prospect respects the director for taking time from his business to assist the bank. "If it means that much to him, it must be a good bank," is the likely reaction.

Spouses of directors and officers may be the most under-utilized resource in our industry. But they cannot help unless they know what we are trying to do. At a retreat of a South Texas bank one spouse brought forward an idea that paid for the whole weekend. Why not include them?

Directors and their spouses are also a powerful marketing influence by doing what one CEO asked, "Talk about the good things in public." What do you have: location, service, history, capital, board, management? Make a list. Directors can make it and agree or disagree. That is a good discussion in itself. If a bank has ten directors and ten spouses, that is 20 contact points a day. Think how many contacts that is in a day, a week, or a month. Each is an opportunity to say something good about the bank. Spouses, including spouses of bank officers and employees, can do a big ambassadorial service. My wife influenced business I could not have touched because I had little contact with her friends. This approach can be made with ease and dignity. Spouses, especially, can smooth ruffled feelings and offer the way for the bank to make amends.

If the bank has "retreats" with directors and staff, spouses can be invited to attend. If they are not informed, they can not explain what the bank is doing or get the prospect in contact with the proper banker.

What should the director do if he hears something that genuinely disturbs him? I asked T. C. Frost, Chairman of Cullen/Frost Bankshares in Texas and of Frost National Bank, San Antonio, who serves on many boards. Tom says in that case he would first seek a one-on-one conference with the CEO. Then, if he did not get a satisfactory answer, he would decide if the issue is important enough to take to the board.

Not every contact will be favorable. If there is dissatisfaction, the director can help save the business, and it is so much easier to save than to replace.

As a consultant, I often hear that most employees would be afraid to pass suggestions directly up to their bosses. Frequently they just do not feel they are on the team. They just work there. The best way to harness potential enthusiasm is to get employees in the know. They want to see evidence that they count. Every one has a marketing role to play and should know what it is, its importance, and how to fill it. But to play on the team, they must believe in the team.

One large bank took an anonymous survey of employee attitudes and found that more than three-fourths would not recommend the bank to their friends, and more than half did not even bank with the institution themselves!

This bank put on a program to sell to their employees and was very successful.

One banker said his best marketing idea is "keeping what we have and then trying for more." To play their part, all employees must see the *customer connection* in what they do.

When I was a CEO I went with another officer of our bank to make a call on a big prospect whom we both knew. When we told him the purpose of the call he reached in his desk drawer and pulled out a letter from a large bank. He had been their customer for 25 years. The letter was from the credit department. It simply said he owed them a financial statement and used the kind of brusque banker wording that is too often seen in routine communications. It did not thank him for doing business there for a quarter of a century. Nor did it note that he did not owe them any money at this time, and they were simply maintaining their ability to serve him. I do not know how many people he had shown that letter to. I do not know how many letters of this kind their credit department had sent to the bank's good customers. Probably the CEO did not know either, for I am sure that he would have stopped them.

Alice L. DeSousa, Senior Vice President of the Bank of New Hampshire Corporation, says, "There are two groups of people in any bank. Those who serve the customer and those who serve those serving the customer."

We left with the prospect's business. The officer who had handled that account for about 25 years probably had no idea why he lost it so quickly. Everybody in the bank must realize that *keeping business* is an important part of their job. In good marketing, bank employees in the credit department develop leads and refer them to the proper department. In some cases, selected employees work after hours on telemarketing campaigns. Incentive compensation is a part of all of this. Anyone who has tried to sell bank services will realize how hard it is to get new customers, and they will work harder to keep those they have.

If two officers, whose time is costing $87.00 an hour each (counting everything), spend two hours talking to a customer over an expensive lunch, it must be part of a productive program. If you have a calling program, consider how to screen prospects and use the big guns on the best targets.

When I started a new company after retirement, I was spending a big part of our income and time selling. I had to get more results to stay in business. Developing a marketing budget helped. That will also help a bank. Include not just what is being spent on advertising, but the costs of officer calls, the annual meeting, the annual report, all fees and charges that are refunded, and anything else connected with selling and keeping customers. Do not be surprised if it is three times as much as you thought. That drives home the realization that our selling efforts *must get results*.

Building And Maintaining A Customer Base

There is little use for the bank to make a marketing effort if it is not prepared to give good service to keep the business it has. One bank I am familiar with had the largest officer-calling program I have ever seen in proportion to the bank—and it was effective. They were bringing in business. However, when prospects or old customers wanted to do business, there was nobody minding the store. The secretary would respond to telephone calls with, "He is out of the bank," or "He is in a meeting." Getting the barriers down means being ready and able to do business—and at the customer's convenience.

Check the competition. At the same time, look at yourself through the customer's eyes. That is the hardest part.

A bank CEO said, "We had 26 officers and employees. I gave each $105.00 to go to a competitor and buy a cashier's check payable to our bank. The $5.00 paid the charges. These contacts were with the customer's exchange and collection department. The employee was to report (at our next employee meeting) whether anyone solicited their account, how they were greeted, and how the competitor bank and its employees looked. This helped us to realize that *this is the way our customers see us.* We saw not only our competitors but ourselves in a new light, through the customer's eyes. The whole effort cost only $130.00 to pay the $5.00 charge on the checks. *And not one of our competitors solicited the account!" My, my, there are untold opportunities in bank marketing.* Consider the exchange and collection department as a potent source of new business.

Marketing is long range. Today's sales effort may not make a profit this month, but through the years to come the profit can be great indeed. This needs to be explained to directors and stockholders.

The good marketing bankers are also profit makers. They know how to hold down costs without accepting slipshod performance. Good marketers take a long-term view; usually planning a strategy over several years—not around a month, a quarter, or a year.

The best marketers also share a strong sense of teamwork. One fine marketer described his as a "family atmosphere." The banker who is slow in answering a loan request or sits around waiting for a good prospective borrower to come to him, will not survive in the top marketing institutions. Executives who make points at headquarters by cutting expenses in disregard of employee morale, or slashing training with no concern for service and increased risk; or saving expenses by letting the physical plant deteriorate, all the while ignoring the level of real customer activity, may be highly regarded for a while, but this will catch up with them.

Another comment from Len Huck: "Bankers are doing more planning on where the bank wants to be, and we have moved marketing from advertising and promotion to the more

substantive issues of bank objectives. But we
do not yet face the competitive environment
with a realization that marketing is not just a
sales campaign, but the way we live our daily
lives as marketers."

PART TWO

55 Ideas From Some Of Banking's Best Marketers

1

Richard Cathie

Executive Vice President
Cape Cod Bank & Trust Company
Hyannis, MA

The American Bankers Association and some state associations publish books on new opportunities available to banks as restrictions fall. Some of these will seem "un-bankerlike," but credit cards and loans on oil reserves in the ground seemed to be so as well only a few years ago. Today, they are widely accepted.

❝ A bank must make a commitment to quality. Mr. & Mrs. America are looking for quality and service and getting less of it all the time.

❝ The public thinks of us (financial institutions) as homogeneous. To be different, we must give the market services where we can *enhance the product*. For example, we all have the convenience of drive-up banks. Could we dispense video movies from the latest most popular list and charge the customer's account $4.00? And consider all the people who are filling out medicare forms. Perhaps our customer has a semi-invalid mother doing this. These forms could be dropped off at a single branch and processed with the customer paying with either hard or soft dollars.

"Many of our customers go to Florida in winter. Could we select the best home-alarm system and market it to our customers, providing a lower monthly rate if they opened an account and let us charge the monthly fee?

"Most of our customers have valuable things to protect. Would they like for one of our officers to go into their home and make a video copy of the contents, with us providing a letter to the insurance company that in the event of loss, this information can be obtained from our bank? They certainly don't want someone coming in to make this record who will perhaps say later 'Boy, you should see that stamp collection.' Banks of the future must be flexible and real market-driven operations.

"I am not sure how many of these things can be done now, but I believe someday, many of them."

The creative banker will look for opportunities that fit his market. There is an abundance of opportunity to provide financial service. This is true even in a slow economy, but the prudent banker will separate the good choices from the bad.

With federal regulators urging expansion of banks' powers and states leading the way, financial institutions should consider what opportunities fit their market and their strengths. Before entering a new area, board and management should ask, "Are we equipped to do this?" If not, get ready and enter slowly.

Mr. Cathie's community on Cape Cod is made up largely of retirees, many of whom keep $75,000 to $100,000 on deposit. Cape Cod has 180,000 year-round residents served by 20 financial institutions with 100 branches. All the big Boston banks are there, with one financial institution for every 1,800 people. Mr. Cathie's bank, Cape Cod Bank & Trust Company, has $525 million in assets, is doing 30 percent of the commercial loan business in the area, and is *earning 1.8 on assets*. They have stressed adaptability. Cathie is among many bankers today looking for new services, many of them simple, which will differentiate and enrich the bank's image in the mind of the customer.

Bankers are creating services with the objective of bringing people into the bank. There is recognition that more people now use services with automatic features, for example, overdraft loans, loan-by-phone, and automatic teller machines. If home banking becomes popular fewer people will need to come into the bank for routine services. This makes each customer's visit to the bank more of an event, and the good marketers will really use these opportunities.

2

Harry Webb

Senior Vice President
First National Bank of Phillips County
Helena, AK

Gone are the times when the customer must rearrange his schedule to meet the "bankers hours." People who succeed in the financial services area will work hard and there are always the community and social demands.

Before you check out of a hotel, there is a form asking you to rate the service. More banks are getting nerve enough to do a similar thing.

❝ We offer personal planning services and investment services to our customers. We extended hours, working from 8:00 A.M. to 6:00 P.M. weekdays and 9:00 A.M. to 2:00 P.M. on Saturdays. Every officer in the bank works every fifth Saturday, and no one works more than every fourth Saturday.

❝ Our bank has redefined job reporting. My background is that of a banker who learned marketing. People in the bank who make most of the customer contacts were reporting to operations officers. Now they all report to me.

❝ We select customers to 'shop' our bank and rate the employees from a standpoint of using the customer's name, smile, personal remarks, and efficient and satisfactory service. Any employee who gets 85 or more is rewarded.

"Our bank hires employees from a standpoint of personality, flexibility, and customer relations orientation and train them in the system. All raises are based on merit with nothing for inflation or longevity.

"In this process we have saved about $65,000 (annually) in salary costs even after going to extended hours."

Mr. Webb's bank has regular biannual performance reviews based on an agreed-upon job responsibility description. When corrections have been made the notation is removed from the personnel file "unless it has to do with audit."

In a few fine institutions, the performance review process results in everybody knowing the objectives of the bank and what part the department and the employees themselves are to play. Each person can have personal objectives, including selling and personal improvement.

One bank has a one-on-one training for supervisors in "Service Plus," which the superior is responsible for. Even the most crusty supervisor will absorb something of a service philosophy when he has to teach it.

Clearly, First National does at least some coaching and counseling during performance reviews. And remember, it is a two-way street. The employee should be able to express himself fully.

Coaching should be positive training: "This is how we want the job done." Counseling is aimed at changing behavior or providing direction. The ability of supervisors to do both coaching and counseling has more to do with reducing turnover than any other factor. The open, nonthreatening, two-way communication possible at performance review time creates an ideal opportunity. But how many times has an employee received a series of satisfactory ratings only to be fired soon after? I know a CEO who got a raise on Tuesday and was fired the following Friday, although there was nothing new in his performance.

3
Lowell Smith, Jr.

CEO and President
First State Bank
Rio Vista, TX

Try getting one of these Pioneer accounts away from First State! As one CEO said, "Keeping the customers you have is the best marketing idea of all."

❝ One of our best ideas has been our pioneer account. It has a picture of the first cabin in this county, and the logo reads 'Pioneers together.' People who have an account for three years or more get this on their checks. *Some of our customers have as many as 50 years on their checks.*

❝For the Texas Sesquicentennial, we commissioned an artist to do 19 historical paintings. These were incidents that occurred in our area. One scene is of a pioneer who was mistakenly killed by the Spaniards as a spy. The artist, George Hallmark, became Texas Artist of the Year. The pictures hang in the bank and over 4,000 school tours have been

People are interested in the history of their communities. A bank that has played a part in that history should emphasize it. Sometimes when an institution is merged the new people are so anxious to shoot up their own rockets that they obliterate the laudable contributions of the past.

"Banks and bankers need to capture the uniqueness of their communities and be a part of it," Stretch says. "We have developed also a cookbook called *Cow Pasture Cooking,* **to which our customers contribute their family recipes. [First State calls itself 'The bank in the cow pasture' because the town is only 460 people and the bank is $127 million in total footings.] We have sold about 30,000 of these. They are widely used for Christmas gifts."**

held explaining each picture and the area depicted. Every year we send out a Thanksgiving card with one of the historical scenes. They are greatly appreciated."

To get to Rio Vista, drive south of Fort Worth through Cleburne and around a bend. You may miss the town, but look to the right and there you will spot a big bank, truly in a cow pasture. These are rock-solid bankers. Lowell "Stretch" Smith is a past president of the Texas Bankers Association, and Mr. Smith and his employees take advantage of every sound marketing opportunity.

They have penetrated the Cleburne market (15 miles to the north) with installment loans, mostly to lower-to-middle wage earners. As this experience shows, your market area can be expanded by true expertise and does not have to be the same for every service. Under many circumstances, in Texas a bank in one county cannot compete effectively in the next county. But some lenders with extensive experience in a special market niche, and backed by outstanding ability to keep track of customers and administer their loans, have been successful in making loans to customers thousands of miles away. Management and board should define what area can be served competitively and safely. Giving a copy to the regulators might avoid "out of territory" questions later.

Lenders who have tried to do business in markets they could not possibly know have suffered terribly. The "nationwide participation lending" involving loan brokers and inexperienced and practically unknown lead lenders is a prime example. A financial institution should ask before going into a new territory or offering a new lending activity, "Do we really know what we are doing in this and can we compete?"

4

John M. Lewis

President
Bank of Fayetteville
Fayetteville, AR

The time to get people who care about serving the customer and the community is during the hiring process. In many institutions there is an atmosphere that speaks to you when you enter. I recently returned a small purchase to Wal-Mart. The "greeter" met me at the door and made it as easy and quick as possible for me to return the item. My son and I stayed to buy $50.00 more in merchandise.

**" ** Some banks have overreacted by making everybody in the bank a salesperson. We want some technicians. But for new accounts and tellers, we try to hire people who like people, and then we train them technically.

"
Exhibit in your community that you care. If you do care, it will sooner or later be transferred into business development.

"
We are forming a community development corporation which has unique advantages. We will use it to improve areas of need. For example, we can buy run-down houses or commercial property, renovate them, and sell them to help redevelop an area.

"We use our board in important community roles. On opening day of our new bank, our directors rolled out a red carpet. It was huge. We had sold $4 million in stock to 344 people.

"We provide lots of training for our board. They help set strategies and objectives. Many people connected with banking say, 'It is not fun anymore.' But we have fun, and it is transmitted to our staff and customers. People who have fun show it and they do a better job."

Frank Easterlin, President of First National Bank, Louisville, Georgia, uses the example, "Each spring, for the past 20 years, we have provided 1,000 azalea plants to the local garden club. The club uses our parking lot over the weekend to sell the plants at bargain prices. Our costs are remitted. The Garden Club makes several hundred dollars, the community is enhanced, and we get a lot of mileage from it."

The Bank of Fayetteville opened in June of 1987. After 15 months it had $40 million in total footings with four thousand accounts. This growth is based on customer and community orientation. *The bank is making money.*

Mr. Lewis takes every opportunity to stress community orientation. A historic building was converted into the main bank building and got the preservation people involved. An old railroad station was converted to a branch.

On advertising, John emphasizes, "All of us are bombarded with a thousand to 15 hundred advertisements every day. We want to do things that are audacious and innovative. When we first put in time and temperature, we bought a double-page ad and simply said: 'Please dial 521-TIME.' We received 5,000 phone calls the first day. Those who dialed got the time *and* the message."

5

Keith Patten

President and CEO
Camden National Bank
Camden, MA

To reward performance may provoke objections that it is not "bankerlike." Plans should be balanced and permit wide participation. Avoid plans that recognize only earnings and center on one or two people. The bank in Dallas that made the highest return on assets one year, failed the next. The CEO received his bonus right up to the time the regulators closed them.

❝ We keep our overhead down by employing fewer people who work harder. We share our profits with our employees. To survive and grow, banks must provide excellent service at low prices. This is not difficult with the help of a profit-sharing plan with our employees.

❝For example, if our peer group average return on assets is 1.1 and we get 1.2, each of our employees gets one week's salary as a bonus. This year we expect to earn 1.7 and each employee will get *six weeks salary as a bonus.*

❝We are a conservative bank with low charge offs and our loan demand is strong because of the quality of our people, especially our loan officers.

"We have gained 10 percent of market share (in our primary counties) in the last five years."

Profit-sharing plans can stimulate employee effort, but people must see how their performance affects profit and how they can do the job in a way that makes a bigger contribution. If the bank does not attain its goals, that should be reflected in reduced or eliminated profit sharing, otherwise the financial incentive to perform is lost.

There is strong evidence that paying employees and officers more, based on performance, improves profit. A key reason is it attracts and holds good, experienced people. They produce, please customers, and hold down mistakes and losses. To reward performance, senior executives must know what good performance is.

Some banks have a "profit sharers meeting," which is similar to the stockholders meeting and is held at about the same time. This recognizes that bank employees really have more invested (their lives) than most stockholders. This meeting is a good place to discuss how each employee and department can improve next year's profit and, thus, their own.

Although Camden National Bank has its main office in a town of 4,700 people, it has branches in some towns that are more populous. *They have doubled in size every four years for the last twelve years, and look at the profit!*

6
John Brown

Executive Vice President
Ocean Street Bank
Neptune Beach, FL

Employees and officers represent us in the bank and in the community. Why not on the radio? Some ads of this kind, using directors, have been very effective.

❝ *We use our own employees to recommend our bank on the radio.* Our slogan is 'Our commitment is to you,' and the advertising statements are built around this. I write the statements and the employee has 25 or 30 from which to choose. For example, the president may say, 'We are constantly building a better bank around you. Your needs. Your financial future.' Our loan officer says, 'I can help you get the loan you need. . . .' Another one of our bankers says, 'We are not just bankers, but part of the community. We live here too.' Credibility is high. We have had calls from people saying, 'How come nobody from my office has been on the radio?'

Low turnover boosts service, cuts costs, and is a sign of good management. Any bank or department can establish a turnover target. This goal, through mutual agreement, can be included in the manager's job description.

The troops cannot take us where we are going unless they know where that is. In too many financial institutions the board, stockholders, or employees do not know what the objectives are, or their part in them. Everyone has a right to wonder—does management know?

" We have an ESOP (Employee Stock Ownership Plan) that makes it attractive for the employees to stay. We also have an unusual pay scale and low turnover.

" If somebody is doing a good job, we ask them to come to the office and say, 'Here's $500. We appreciate what you have been doing.' The amount goes with the level of the job. But this is not just for management. If the janitor is doing a good job, he gets the same recognition, not just in money, but in staff meetings—and they get it that week.

" We have low turnover and high productivity. Our employees know a lot about the company and what we are trying to do."

John's is an independent bank that has captured 41 percent of the market. He has built this marketing around the idea that customer is king: "Our employees know what products we sell and everybody tells the same story."

A few years ago, many banks had only two products dealing with deposit accounts—regular checking and saving. Now, many have a dozen or more. How many of our employees know those services, who performs them, and what customers need them?

The marketing officer of one large bank said, "We call our competition (not the top echelon) and ask them such questions as 'Do you make home improvement loans, and if so who does it?' He says, 'They don't know.' He added, 'We don't either.' "

This statement was made by a broadly experienced banker: "An informed employee is the best assurance of marketing success." He brings his directors and all officers into a program of education on the services of the bank and why it does what it does. Sometime spouses are included.

A company making medical supplies experienced 100 percent annualized turnover in the most routine, boring, and yet critical, part of the manufacturing operation. It was breaking the company. A new manager of that area reduced this to near zero by taking an interest in the employees. High turnover is generally not inevitable.

Another bank has a "lunch and learn" program where one service is covered each day in the lunchroom. Of course, this could be done any time a group of employees can be gathered. An East Texas bank takes the employees out of the bank in small groups for three days each, to cover not only what the services are, but how to perform them.

Turnover is related to the market (are there better jobs available?) and any unusual occurrences, such as a change in what is expected of the employee. But in some departments, and even whole companies, high turnover has been reduced to almost nothing through better management. If there is a high turnover in an area, we should not take it as inevitable or say it is no worse than others, but find what Peter Drucker calls the "critical factor" and improve.

7

Andy Shepard

Chairman and CEO
Exchange Bank
Santa Rosa, CA

Number of complaints is a good way to judge the quality of service provided by a person or an area. As CEO, I had a few people who worked for us for years without a single customer complaint that reached me.

❝ *We hire contact personnel on the basis of personality, not experience. We bankers have been wrong to hire for experience and then try to teach the employees to be salespeople.*

❝ I was first exposed to this idea at a hotel in Hawaii and brought it back to the bank to put it into effect. It sounded easy, but it was not. We lost good tellers and supervisors who could not handle this change. We had such strict rules that our tellers could not be nice to the customer and still meet the requirements of balancing. So we became more lenient on our cash differences. I used to get calls complaining about our service. Now I get one or two a year. Our bank went from 1.1 to 1.7 return on assets, and we attribute a part of this to the change in attitude."

Andy is past president of the California Bankers Association and a leader in the ABA. He and other bankers realize we cannot continue to bring in only people with orientation to systems and figures and then expect them to become salespeople (or managers) when they get promoted to a different job. He says, "We can teach the fundamentals of banking, but we have not been able to change a person's personality."

The need for balance in people talents applies especially to the board loan committees. We need different viewpoints. Peter Ducker says, "Don't arrive at a conclusion until disagreement is reached."

For the past 2,500 years, efforts have been made to describe people by their primary orientation, and these are well worth study. Most of our directors and top management tend to be action-oriented, "bottom line" people. Those in operations, and frequently in loans, are focused on systems and structure. In earlier years we only tolerated "people" type folks because they were needed in marketing and personnel, and perhaps occasionally as CEO. Idea-oriented people were discouraged in the industry because they were too "far out." They were actually thinking five to ten years in the future!

Banks need people of various skills and orientation. Banks that do not have idea people, who are thinking not just months but years in the future, should get some. The board is a good place to start. These qualities can be found in a city manager or hospital administrator. Not every director needs to be rich or own and operate or head a business. Boards should be broad-based in skills and representative of the community.

8
Smith W. Brookhart III

President and CEO
Ozark Mountain Bank
Branson, MO

More banks are using public relations money in ways that do double duty. For example, one large bank recently announced a very big contribution to help local schools. The favorable effect of this on people in the community can last for years and the good done goes on even after the bank's contribution is forgotten.

❝ Branson has a volunteer library privately supported and run by a very serious group of women. They do bake sales and many other things to raise money. Our bank asked the leaders if we could do something to help raise money for a new building. When they accepted eagerly, we designed a special savings account. For every dollar that went into that account, we gave .01¢ to the library. It was otherwise a normal savings account, but with limited access to assure that we did not get hot money.

❝Our bank took in $7.5 million in new money which provided $75,000 seed money for the library. It was a big beginning. Others joined with their own ideas. The library is now operating in a new 10,000 square foot facility. Our bank generated an immense amount of good will along with the new business."

Mr. Brookhart's bank has $80 million in assets in a county with three banks and three savings and loan associations. The assets in these institutions total about $190 million. Getting such a high market share represents a great marketing job. Branson is located in the lake country of Missouri. This area generates good loan activity and also saving deposits from retirees.

9
Carrol Pruett

President
Midstate Bank
Arroyo Grande, CA

Customers have very strong feelings about going to the same banker, even the same teller. Stressing continued service of bankers with skill and authority is a competitive plus for many banks. "I don't know anybody there anymore" is still the biggest customer complaint and is especially disturbing when the customer sees other major changes.

❝ Our best marketing ideas have been creating and preserving the image of the little town bank in the communities that we serve. We want to deserve this reputation.

❝ Our officers and employees have a visible role in the community. We stress continuity of officers and staff. If a branch manager is doing a good job we like to keep him there and make it worth his while. Many of the major banks in our area are cutting and consolidating. Some have branches where there is no one with lending authority. We find people still want to know the bankers with whom they are dealing."

A Texas customer whose local bank had been acquired by an outside holding company went in for a $10,000 loan to buy a male ostrich. He explained that he already owned females, and ostrich eggs were valuable. After squirming for awhile, the loan officer blurted, "I'm not going to be known as the guy who brought an ostrich loan to committee." The borrower walked across to another bank where he was known to be easily good for $10,000 and is now producing and selling ostrich eggs ... and enjoying his new bank connection.

Sounds like a small bank? Mr. Pruett's organization operates over a 200-mile stretch of California. He says financial institutions that have tried to create "lending hubs" have lost market share, while those that continued to serve the people at the loan officer's desk are gaining.

Throughout these interviews I have found some big banks, often operating offices from distant headquarters, which manage to stay close to their customers, render great service, and are seen as a part of the hometown team. But it is apparent from comments of competitors, and even their own directors and employees' that many other such banks are seen as foreign, or "not us" as the Japanese would say.

Obviously Mr. Pruett's bank begins by not ignoring the issue, but putting it up front and working at the solution. They do not act like outsiders—and so they are not regarded that way.

Keeping the same people is a big part of Midstate's success in meeting this challenge. I do not worry too much that my banker has a boss in a far away city, if the same bank officer is serving me year after year. Recognition of local people's needs and attitudes is vital.

10

Larry Bayliss

Senior Vice President, Advertising and Marketing
Boatman's National Bank
St. Louis, MO

Peter Drucker says our employees (not just in banks) do not feel they are on the team. When an employee is selling the bank's products, they become not only more sales-minded, but more sold themselves. "If Boatman's means people making the difference, I am the difference. I am the team." Imagine having thousands of employees feeling that way!

❝❝ We use testimonial advertising. We took a retail survey of customers and non-customers, and 2,800 responded. *We found they wanted service, for the bank to be responsive, and for themselves, as customers, to be appreciated.* They would shop rates, but that was to be expected. We trained our people to meet these needs and then asked, 'How are we going to tell our customers what Boatman's means?' We felt it meant our slogan: Boatman's, people making the difference.

❝ We have 9,000 employees in Missouri, Illinois, and Tennessee and have had a hundred interviews used in advertising campaigns. We will eventually have three thousand (interviews). Credibility is sky high because these are real employees, unrehearsed, doing all this ad lib. It is done by radio with a bit of newspaper."

Customers of other banks have the same desires as Boatman customers—and here is a big bank that is getting it to them. Big institutions *can* be close to their customers and many are. They just have to try harder.

Employees have a strong tendency to identify with a slogan if they see that management believes it and is relying on employees to really make it come true.

11

Wayne Weidner

President
Bank of Boyertown
Boyertown, PA

A letter followed by a telephone call—this is a good selling sequence. The day of the week the letter and call arrive is also important.

Bankers agree. Training the callers and conveying a message of real interest to the prospect are the keys to telemarketing.

▌▌ When the IRA legislation changed, our bank got in the top ten in the United States in the IRA deposit business (as a percentage of total bank deposits). We offered an above market introductory rate for the first year of the deposit and those dollars stayed with us. This selling was done by direct mail followed by telemarketing. The callers were our own people trained in the way we wanted them trained.

❝ When home equity loans opened up, we offered a below market (loan) rate for the first few months, with a three tier level, depending on the percentage of equity. Again the marketing was by mail, followed by telemarketing."

Mr. Weidner's bank has grown in 26 years from a $20 million institution to more than $500 million! This is some record when the growth is sound, profitable, consistent, and long term. That is the only kind of growth that makes money for stockholders. Fast, mushroom growth has fostered trouble in many financial institutions.

12

Pam Fisher

Senior Vice President
Habersham Bank
Clarksville, GA

In these times of dramatic change, bankers must be better informed—and not just about what is going on in the bank. Customers expect officers to know much more than how to make loans, and bankers must be broadly informed to be good lenders. For example, increased oil production in Saudi Arabia caused main street cafes to close in Odessa, Texas. This hit the banks.

❝ We believe the essence of marketing is *service*. That begins with trained, loyal, and experienced employees.

❝ *Service is something we must deliver, not just talk about. It must go throughout the institution.*

❝ We try to hire people who are friendly and sincerely want to work with our customers. We can teach them the technical aspects of the job. Our training budget is over $100,000 a year and 38 percent of that goes toward college tuition. Our president believes that the better people feel about themselves, the better employees we have. The courses they take at bank expense must be business-related.

"We have started what we call 'the certified professional teller's program.' This takes two to three years to complete and involves financial reward as well as recognition. At one level there is a 20 percent salary increase and at another there is a $500 bonus. There is also an extra week of vacation. Now 82 percent of our tellers participate. Some participate who are not tellers. There is much cross-training and cross-selling.

"Every new employee has an orientation of from a half a day to two days. Our four senior officers talk to them. We talk about policies, what our bank stands for, its mission in the community, and especially about service."

In his seminars, Tom Peters gives his students (executives) time to call their businesses and speak to an employee who has been there less than two weeks. They are instructed to ask "What is unique about our company?" How many of your employees could answer that question? If they cannot they do not feel they are on the team.

How much should a bank spend for training and what kind? Some banks and smaller financial holding companies try to hire already trained people for all the most important jobs. Doing this robs other banks, strips the industry, increases salary costs, and is seen as depriving long-time employees of opportunity. However, sometimes it has worked. One holding company president who follows the program of hiring proven outsiders in upper level positions says, "I know somebody has paid a big ticket for that."

If the bank cannot keep the people, the money spent training them goes for the benefit of others. It is harder now for banks to convince employees they will have a job as long as they perform well. These people read the newspaper. Many layoffs are announced in the headlines. In our Texas area, banks are no longer able to hire the top graduates of the local colleges and universities. Yet today's, and especially tomorrow's, bankers must be more broadly equipped than ever before. So where are we going to get these paragons to play important roles in our banks and communities in the future?

One banker who has brought his institution through rough times with a profit every year cited the quality of his staff, especially in lending. He noted that the woman in charge of commercial lending joined the bank years ago as a collateral clerk and received the benefit of a lot of training both in the bank and in banking schools.

One relatively new $25 million bank in a town of 12,000 people competing with two larger, older banks is spending $40,000 a year on training. The last time I checked, they were making 1.7 on assets in a tough market. They have made their point through performance.

Where are we going to get the outstanding employees of the future? This banker answered that question, "We must train those we have." That means in most banks, stepping up training. It also means hiring more people of high potential, and selecting and promoting managers with very high potential.

Our training must recognize what a broad field banking is and the important role bankers are expected to play. Many must learn more about not only marketing, but decision making, communication, coaching, counseling, motivation, and much more.

The training should prepare the employee for the future, not just the present. Sometimes we are providing training on auditing to an auditor who will soon be moving into the controllers office. It is vital for supervisors to know the employee's probable career course before scheduling training and to have agreement on the benefits to be gained and check results. One banker says that, before he sends anyone to a school or conference, he meets with that person to ask, "What do you hope to learn?" Later he asks, "What did you bring back and put to work for us?"

The Habersham Bank has been building its reputation since 1904. As a bank of about $125 million, it is the largest bank in a very competitive market. There are 30,000 people in the county.

13

William McConnell

Chief Executive Officer
Park National Bank
Newark, OH

" We have been very effective in telemarketing. It was hard for me to accept because I don't like to be called at home. For a long time, we had been trying to get a software program that would permit us to extend a real line of credit to consumers that they could run up and down. The change in the tax law (making home equity loans tax-deductible) gave us this opportunity. We marketed it with the slogan that said, 'This is the last loan you will ever need.' That was a good story but it needed to be told. We looked at our own customers and then went to the courthouse to see who had substantial home equity.

"Our people are awfully good. We close at 5:00 P.M., buy these teams some pizza, and by

6:30 many are making telephone calls. After our caller suggests the idea, he says, 'If this interests you, let's meet at the bank and talk about it.' The prospect may say he works during the day and so our caller says, 'Could you come at 8:00 Thursday night and I will have a loan officer there to meet with you.' We pay our employees a bonus when they are able to make an appointment. However, it isn't just the money. *It is doing something important and being part of the team.*

" We sell other services by telephone. If a customer has paid out an auto loan, we call him and tell him we appreciate that, and when he is ready for another car, we will certainly be here to serve him.

" Also, we specialize in lending to small businesses. Often the small business is getting along just fine with a big bank, but for some reason, lose their loan officer. A small business owner doesn't just want to duck into a branch somewhere but wants somebody to talk to. We tell him, "We'll help you with your business."

Any small business owner is proud of what has been built and wants the bank to recognize it. Our bank sponsored "big customer luncheons." The customers provided the program by telling how they started their business and handled problems. They love that and the bank can introduce these customers to more bank officers. The "I don't know anyone there anymore" syndrome will not apply.

When I hear examples like Mr. McConnell's, I overcome my resistance to telemarketing too. Park National has a reason for the call and they use their own employees. The telephone message is meaningful. The customer also knows the person calling is not a boiler-room professional, but an employee staying at work late to make this call.

When we have located the prospect and know what he needs, the sale is half made. Some banks have the capacity to make a "need analysis" before the first call on the prospect.

14

Biff Motley

Executive Vice President
Premier Bank Corp., Inc.
Baton Rouge, LA

Markets are all different. That means the banks that serve them should be different too, even if they belong to the same banking organization.

❝ We have our "hot points" program. We are in eight markets. We watch closely the interest rates on certificates in those markets. When we see the opportunity to acquire funds which will not raise the rate on our whole deposit structure, we move in with something like a "blue plate special" to get a better market share on a quick-in and quick-out basis. We might be able to offer a six month certificate of deposit in Lake Charles and at the same time a 3 month "mini-jumbo" in Monroe.

❝ In Louisiana interest rates are lower than elsewhere because of the economy, but we have many customers inclined to go to treasury securities. This has been a very helpful and creative idea."

Anything that holds down the cost of money enables a bank to meet the competition and still improve spread. It also enables the institution to get high quality loans at a very competitive rate, thus serving the most desirable customers.

But price is not enough. The banker still needs to say "your business is important to us." The borrower who feels insecure in the relationship knows if the bank "pulls the plug" he is in for a lot of trouble even if his statement, income, and collateral justify his loan. This is especially true in areas with a shaky economy. Many good borrowers prefer to maintain relationships with more than one bank.

15

John Russell

Vice President
Bank One
Columbus, OH

Ms. Linda Lockhart, Director of Marketing for Dollar Drydock in New York, a $5 billion institution with 23 branches covering a wide area, says the idea of the financial marketplace center works in a community of 5,000 as well as in New York City. Services they offer include travel, real estate, insurance, brokerage, and mortgage loans, as well as usual banking services. Linda says they provide information assistants who "don't have a chair" and her best success in hiring has been with people who have been waiters or actors.

❝ The development of the Affinity Credit Card Program and Joint Issue Credit Card Program was one of our best marketing ideas. The first was with Merrill Lynch.

❝ We installed the first automatic teller machine in the United States in 1970. That started a revolution in banking.

❝ Our emphasis now is the introduction of a financial marketplace center. This will incorporate up to ten financial related services, such as stock brokerage, trust, tax service and legal service, travel agent and others, as well as all the regular banking services. Those that can't legally be provided by the bank will be provided space on a leased basis. This will be a sort of mini-shopping center providing banking services."

The great record of Bank One and its leadership in marketing speaks for itself.

Institutions of various sizes in different "kinds of communities" are working with the "financial center" concept. Federal savings banks have the advantage of being able to actually be in all these businesses. Some banks rent the space on a share of the profit's arrangement.

A bank serving several small communities in Georgia is designing all its branches to have the financial services related to banking, such as brokerage, insurance, and travel, officing in the front part of the lobby. Another banker working on the financial center concept says, "The supermarkets all put the milk and other staples in the back of the store. This compares to putting the tellers in the rear so the customer must pass and see the other services."

16

Bill Watson

Chairman and CEO
Bank of Saint Joseph
St. Louis, LA

Employees who have fun do a better job. One CEO said his best marketing idea is an employee's day, "when everyone wears informal clothes." Employees are happier and react more enthusiastically to the customer.

66 We have tried to get sophisticated enough in our computer equipment to bring up any group of customers and send them a letter. For example, we can send letters to all our customers who are members of a country club and not members of any other organizations we select, or vice versa. These letters include first name saluations which takes away any suggestion that they were "computerized."

66 For example, we have football fans who follow the (New Orleans) Saints and the (LSU) Tigers. We offered (these fans) Saints and Tigers CDs which were about 15 basis points below the market, but provided that after every game the team won, the customer got an in-

crease of 5 basis points. We sold about $600,000 of these and they were seen as interesting to people. We have a lot of fun with our business.

"We try to take a rifle shot at our market. First we had to get our system in place, then think of the ideas—the hardest part!"

A rifle shot is the only kind most small banks can afford. And they must hit the target often to stay in business and gain market share.

The comment about having fun is BIG. People have fun when they feel secure and happy in what they are doing and are eager to do more of it. The result: higher morale and better performance. Customers sense that attitude the moment they walk in.

On the other hand, dour employees convey a negative message. The worst example is the senior executive who shuffles through the lobby with a frown and holds his head down or stands on the mezzanine looking like a cloud of doom!

17

Doug Campbell

Chairman and CEO
State Savings Bank of Caro
Caro, IL

" About four years ago we hired Jud Moran to conduct a market audit of our bank. Jud spent several days in the bank and in the community doing research. He then prepared a detailed report which contained numerous suggestions and recommendations, most of which we have since implemented. This got us started.

" Our first major task was to replace our in-house computer system. We did this by investing in an IBM System 36 and purchasing software. We now are able to get the information we need to offer our customers the bank services they need.

"We offer 'life line' accounts to seniors, encourage them to adopt direct deposit of their social security checks, come in the bank to just visit with their peers, have coffee, read current periodicals, newspapers, etc. Also, we have developed a wide range of new services including discount brokerage, trust/estate planning, credit and debit cards, an automatic teller machine at our main office, home equity lines of credit, etc.

"The production of an annual report, which is now widely distributed to local business people and various treasurers, has also helped us to promote the market for our bank stock."

"Who is willing to own stock in our bank?" is a growing question, especially where large stockholders want to reduce their holdings. Enlarging the stockholder base is a big job, but referrals from a stockholder group can make this very worthwhile. Try small lunches to keep stockholders informed and interested.

Mr. Campbell's is a $55 million bank that has had steady growth. He says, "We work on getting referrals through local accountants and attorneys and, in consequence, do not have an accountant or attorney on our board."

Information. Banks have more than others. One banker said, "When a commercial credit company enters the market, the first thing they do is buy a book of business to get leads and information."

The reason many banks do a poor job of following on the abundance of prospects is that banks have too many! Any method of gathering leads without a system, objectives, and follow-through will bog down in sheer numbers. Executives must focus and follow up on the high priority possibilities.

The annual report deserves special attention. It impresses the stockholder or fails to and will be talked about either way. In times of lowered expectations, be candid. The wise CEO will maintain credibility by getting the bad news to the directors and stockholders first, thus avoiding the natural tendency to think these problems can be cured before they attract too much attention.

A CEO in Dallas was able to raise capital from existing stockholders to take advantage of opportunities arising from the sale of failed banks by the FDIC. He did this even when the area was so depressed and there was little market for the stock of most banks. He says this was because he had always given his board and stockholders the bad news as well as the good.

18

Dan Mello

Chairman and President
National Bank of Fairhaven
Fairhaven, MA

One banker said (in the midst of the Texas recession) that his lending officers were so overwhelmed with workouts, they could not give attention to even good new loan requests. That is too bad. When other banks' customers are upset, this is the time for other institutions to reap the harvest.

" We emphasize stability of employees. Frequently, if an officer of one of our competitors is good, he goes to another location, and if he is bad, he gets fired. *So we emphasize to our customers they will have the same officer and we will give a quick turnaround on a loan request.*

" We are now assigning accounts and plan to do more officer calling. Our officer and directors are active in many local organizations, which is an important source of new business. We have a shortage of trained people. I recently hired a senior lender from Texas."

This idea seems simple but is something any bank can do to stabilize customer relationships, especially with borrowers. It is interesting to see the number of bankers who feel the best thing they have to sell (and not just to commercial borrowers) is the sense of all-around security and satisfaction a customer gets from dealing with a banker they know. This applies to all contacts, certainly including tellers.

19

Hudson Mead

President
Texas Commerce Bank
Longview, TX

❝ We had a massive training program to develop a customer service management style for our whole bank. Our retail lenders, tellers, bookkeeping department, all have been reorganized and report through department heads to one marketing-oriented banker. We want all these contact people to know the answers to the customer's questions, such as our rates on new car loans. We want them not only to understand what the other departments do, but be able to do those jobs. We put a lot of emphasis on cross-selling.

❝ *People are out of the bank, about a half dozen at a time, for three days of solid training.* High emphasis is placed on improving our information system in order to get a better profile of our customers. Tying together all the information and using it is at the heart of our marketing program.

"Our "one-plus" program embraces the seven most popular services and reminds our employees of cross-selling opportunities for which we pay incentive compensation. *Our customers now average using 3.97 of our services.*

"Like most other banks in Texas, we need to cut our turnover so the customer feels the sense of being waited on by the same people year after year."

Hiring usually begins by looking for someone with training and skills to fill a particular job. What kind of people are needed, not just to fill today's vacancy, but to fill other important positions and run the bank in the future? Those who are influential in hiring should be thinking about that. The institution cannot be any better than the people it hires and promotes. Loyd Swope, President of the Bank of Lincoln, Lincoln Arkansas, says his best marketing idea is "getting the right people."

This is another example of organization that places customer contact people under an all-around marketing-oriented banker. But marketing effort cannot take the place of real knowledge of what those jobs entail. Banks can lose their shirts in new accounts or the exchange window or wire transfer.

Hudson's bank (a member of Texas Commerce Holding Company) is located in an area which has been hard hit by the decline in oil activity but is making a gradual comeback through diversification. Emphasizing not only the training, but the initial selection of employees, Hudson says, "It's not the cost of employees, but the cost of mediocrity that we cannot afford."

Many bankers have realized the many faceted cost of turnover. Those who are content with saying "We have about the same turnover as everyone else" are on the wrong approach. Something can be done about it, and if we had to report the cost of turnover on the profit and loss statement, something would be done.

20
Lee Tabas

President
Royal Bank of Pennsylvania
King of Prussia, PA

"" Once a month we have a luncheon attended by 15 to 20 people, including half a dozen officers. We go around the room and ask each to tell us about his business, how it started, and so forth. They really like this. They get acquainted with each other and we have the advantage that more of our officers know our good customers and about their businesses. This is a very low-key buffet luncheon. We have a follow-up which is also quite low-key."

Another bank that made *no* follow-up on these luncheons had disappointing results. Lee's low-key follow-up may be the right approach.

Referrals by stockholder customers can produce leads to good business. If your bank has a considerable number of stockholders, try small lunches to keep them boosting their bank, and have a system that asks them for referrals.

Lee's bank makes good profits. It was founded in 1963 and has grown to over $250 million in total resources. He offers some special services to fill particular needs. For example, loans to companies involved in environmental clean-up and improvement. This shows the community that his bank cares. It is a part of a community wide program to identify and work on unmet needs.

There is an abundance of financial needs in any community that only the institution based in that community or a lender who acts like one will meet. These include special projects, such as loans for improvements of the shopping center or purchase and renovation of old homes. These efforts make several kinds of long-term profit for the bank through improving its environment and image, although there might not be an immediate direct profit.

21
Max Wells

Chairman
The Oaks Bank & Trust Company
Dallas, TX

" We acquired our bank from the FDIC. The previous owners had not paid attention to the retail establishment in the community. We formed a new merchants association which now has about 180 members and has brought about a significant change in the environment of the bank, as well as producing much good will and some customers.

" Also our advisory board idea works well. We also have quarterly breakfasts with customers, prospects and bank officers, always having a well-known speaker.

" We make a big deal about talking to people in the teller's line. I do this myself to set an example, especially at crowded times. It's important to be able to say, 'I'm sorry you have to wait.'

"We make at least a monthly contact with our directors outside of the board meeting and in each case ask for referrals."

A director who expressed thoughts about some of the bank's loans to an Executive Vice President was given a lot of rebuttal that "made him feel like a fool." He added, "I'll never do that again." Scratch one source of good outside information for that bank!

Some directors, who are reluctant to speak up in the meetings, will provide wisdom as well as business development help if the CEO calls the director at his place of business. This also builds the relationship and can be a way for the director to speak out on feelings or criticisms he would be reluctant to express in a meeting.

Several years ago Max Wells started a new bank and one of the things he did was "knock on a few doors on the way home." He knew he would not be doing anything else for that 20 or 30 minutes. The prospects' pleasant reactions were, "You came by my house to call on me!" So much for the fear of calling on prospects at home!

22

Jud Moran

Justin L. Moran, Incorporated
Ann Arbor, MI

Tony La Russa, Manager of the Oakland Athletics, says winning pennants in baseball results from "doing things right." Same with us.

" The best marketers I know are not those out there with a handful of balloons. They surround themselves with good people and good products, have an understanding of the market, and whip the daylights out of the competition.

"Understanding the market and having the guts to hire good people, and just doing things right day-in and day-out—this is what makes marketing success.**"**

23

Richard P. Morthland

President
Peoples Bank & Trust Company
Selma, AL

The customer will remember the contact at the hospital much longer than the call made to get him to move some money. After a serious operation I received a call from the chairman of a bank with which I have done a lot of business, and I will never forget it.

The head of a chain of restaurants who operates in 65 markets says, "Each of our markets is different and so each restaurant must be different." Some big banks tried a "cookie cutter" approach and lost local market appeal as well as diversity of input.

❝❝ Each of our directors makes two business development calls a month. And each officer makes four calls. Some officers are not good at making business development calls, but any of them can go by the hospital and say to our customers, 'I hope you get well soon.'

❝ A community bank in a small town, particulary a large community bank in a small town, must serve all parts of the area's life. Since no one segment is large enough to provide a profitable niche, we must be a little bit of everything to everybody.❞

91

"**M**arket segmentation" has become very popular—the new wisdom. But it has many disadvantages, hit squarely by Dick Morthland. The community bank can serve the whole market because they know it so well. A commercial credit company can specialize in one form of lending, for example, on manufactured housing, because they have the whole nation for a market and are equipped to do it well.

Directors can be used on the most important calls. The strongest approach a bank can make to a prospect is for a bank officer and director to call at the prospect's office and say, "We sure would like to have you for a customer."

A successful entrepreneur put it this way: "We know if the bank pulls the plug our business is in danger." This is true because in that particular market where there are few lenders who can or want to handle that type of business. Many commercial borrowers place a feeling of confidence in the lender and his ability to handle the business first in importance, even above interest rate.

Peoples Bank & Trust is one of very few banks I called that mentioned making use of directors in marketing. And their directors make two calls a month! If a bank has twelve directors, that would be 24 calls a month. Think of what that means if carried out year after year. Add to it, if you can, some good ambassadorial service by the spouses and you have a powerful part of the team in place.

Mr. Morthland also emphasizes that his bank sells a feeling of security. Peoples Bank and Trust will have the same officers and employees and will continue to serve the customers in the same competent way. Borrowers and business customers especially prize this sense of security and will pay more to get it. We are not talking about the big company with assured credit at the prime rate. Many bankers have long-time customers who remember "You were there when I needed you" and have a high sense of loyalty.

Consistency and *continuity* are two of the greatest words in banking. It is important they be reflected in loan policy and the attitudes of committees and loan officers.

Every banker, especially those making commercial loans, is selling a sense of security. A common expression heard is that "all money is the same," but it is not if the borrower suddenly cannot get it, or senses he might not be able to because of a change of bank policy, personnel, or ownership. Many customers of banks that have gone through the FDIC and on to new ownership have experienced this phenomenon when those loans have gone on to the FDIC or been put in the workout bank.

24

Bryan O'Connor

President and CEO
Crown Bank
San Antonio, TX

❝ We offer a cash award for every new account (referred by an employee). In a previous bank connection an exchange teller brought in 21 to 22 new accounts every month by cross-selling those who came to her window."

The importance of the exchange window is often overlooked. It can be a great source of new business. But as one banker put it, "Every employee must be responsible for their primary job component." The people in the exchange window have heavy responsibilities that can cost the bank a lot of money if not carried out. However,without lapsing in their primary duties, there can still be many referrals coming from the exchange window.

25
Fred Landiss

Vice President, Marketing
Dominion Bank
Clarksville, TN

❝ We have cornered the female banking market in Clarksville. This is through our 'First Ladies' (we were First National Bank for 123 years). This is for women that have a balance of over $50 thousand with us. We have them to luncheons in small groups. There is a small grey membership card with the state flower on it and they receive a benefit package that includes free checking, free cashiers checks, and money orders. We have 450 members and expect to add another 150 next year. *They currently have $40 million on deposit.* The informal research on this was done by just sitting in our lobby and observing who was doing business with us. Most were women.

"We have seminars called 'Money Matters and So Do You.' The focus of these programs is financial. But the 'So Do You' is about personal development. For example, a very successful female personality may tell how she succeeded in business. We sell 275 tickets to each of these at $20 and the tickets go quickly because the programs are well planned and developed. Between speakers (at each of these seminars) we promote one bank service. It is great public relations, an inexpensive way to reach new customers, and costs the bank very little.

Appeal to groups is a great and growing market in banking. Our own bank's Emerald Club (55 and over) has 5,000 members and is growing. Members of these groups sell their friends. "Come with me to the luncheon." But do not start unless you intend to pay attention. If neglected, these groups can become very dissatisfied.

"There is another series, 'Seminars for Anyone.' For each of these we charge $1.00 for a non-customer. This has an effect because people don't want to be considered outsiders.

"Our travel program (for these groups) has been highly successful. Trips are arranged from something on the Cumberland River to travel to London. For three years every trip has been a 'sell-out.' We also have a 55-plus group, retired military group, and we are now developing 'young entrepeneur' organization for young business people between 25 and 40. We can't start all these groups at one time, but we intend to add one group every year. Each must have programs that are continuous and ongoing to be successful."

Generally members of these "mature market" clubs pay for most of what they get. The key is that they belong, somebody is paying attention to them and there are exciting things to do. Select a creative and compassionate person to run it. It is also fine if members of the group can have a special place to drink coffee,

Deposit Guaranty National Bank, a $3.5 billion institution with 129 locations in Mississippi, offers a mature market program. Wallace McMillan, Senior Vice President says, "We started in February 1988 with our 'Guaranty Gold' program. It includes a no service charge checking account and a package of other services to people 55 and over. This includes travel, educational programs, driving courses, and so forth. We marketed this by direct response TV . . . The spokesman explained the account and offered a free travel atlas to those who called the 800 number. We were able to give our branches 1,200 qualified leads and after one year had 3,500 members . . . ."

read correct publications, and visit together. By allowing club members to select the board or leadership candidates, a sense of ownership is developed.

Some banks have been successful in group banking with teachers, young people (first-time customers), and others. John Nicholson, President, Peoples State Bank, Henderson, Texas, has Teacher Appreciation Banking, a "First Generation" account (for people 55 and over) and a "Starter Club" for young people. They are getting sons and daughters of people who have been banking at the older banks for generations.

Other banks have offered lectures, birthday lunches, cocktail parties, and trips to the local art gallery. One group has a board that selects what they want to do from a smorgasbord of opportunities.

Ross Greenwood, CEO of a bank in Salado, Texas (and former president of the Texas Bankers Association), emphasized the success of their programs for senior citizens. He calls this his most successful marketing idea and recommends it to many banks that have a market among older people.

If you are young and active in business you may have too many invitations; when you retire, it is different. Retired or semi-retired people are looking for something to do and social, educational, and travel programs attract them.

26

Carl Erskine

President
First National Bank
Anderson, IN

New laws, making geographic expansion more possible, have become very significant for institutions of all sizes. There are expanding opportunities to cross state lines and for merging of different types of organizations. Many of the institutions that went through the FDIC wringer became branches.

❝ I am still seeking new opportunities by opening branches in adjacent counties as recently permitted by Indiana Law. This permitted us to participate in the big growth coming out of Indianapolis toward the Northeast. In 1986 we joined with six other community banks to form the Star Financial Group, a mid-Indiana holding company with $550 million in assets.

❝Our current emphasis is on making and selling mortgages and retaining the servicing."

Baseball fans will remember Carl as an all time great Brooklyn Dodger pitcher wearing number 17. As a banker, he is still pitching. His was a $5 million bank that moved in the early '60s from a small town in the county to Anderson, Indiana. Since then, it has grown to $135 million while competing with two well-established banks and large savings and loan associations in a city of 65,000. His bank is getting stronger in commercial loans, but he still has a major orientation as a consumer bank.

Carl is building upon the old while establishing the new. Some financial institutions have made the mistake of giving up the old before proving out the new. And why give up the old at all if it is still working well? One banker emphasizes "product extension." That is building on what has already proved successful. I like that.

27

Kay Robinson

Senior Vice President/Marketing Director
National Bank of Commerce
Starkville, MI

Being "the oldest" institution in the market was important years ago. That desire of customers for strength is back in full force. In areas of economic distress, banks that are stronger, safer, and more consistently profitable have gained new respect and have had an inflow of new business.

❝ Every three years we do a consumer survey. The latest one showed that the consumer basically sees no difference between banks. *Therefore we must create the difference.* We are the only locally based Starkville bank, we are 100 years old, and we continue to offer a superior level of service. When out-of-town banks take over, service sometimes declines. Customers who are accustomed to a more localized approach then shop for a bank that will provide what they want.

❝We have been nationally recognized as one of the 175 safest banks in the country. Using the mailing list for the American Assocation of

103

Retired Persons, we sent letters emphasizing our strength along with progressiveness.

Use your stockholders in marketing as they can be a great source of input. If some actions of the bank, or its executives, are causing unpopularity, stockholders will tell you. But "somebody must be listening."

" In our shareholders, we have a large advantage over the bigger holding companies because their shareholders are a bit more removed. We do a 'shareholders update' telling them what we are about to do and why, and (do) the same for our employees. We are also able to emphasize that our bank has been consistently among the most profitable in the state.

" The effectiveness of our marketing program is due to our CEO who is dedicated to it and does not cut the budget in the middle of the year. I start every year with a zero-based budget, look at the marketplace, decide what we need to do, and how many dollars we need to do it. We don't necessarily get all those dollars, but we get a good part of them, and we don't have to change our program if profit declines. *When market share is going down or sales decline, that's the time to add to marketing.*

" In our bank, marketing is something that pervades the whole institution. As a part of our planning, every employee writes out his personal goals to help fulfill the bank's mission.

" We have just opened a grocery store branch which is really taking off. We learned that we are no different from the deli or the bakery. I just had a meeting with some of our employees in the grocery store branch who complained that potential customers had been rude. I said, 'Now you see what the poor grocery store employees have to put up with.' When you can open a CD at 7:00 on Saturday night you know you are doing something right. Our customers tell us, 'I can't get to your bank during regular hours because of my work. This is the greatest thing that ever happened to me.'"

Opening supermarket branches has become a popular idea in some parts of the country. Some banks are now planning to open in stores with wide, but selective, appeal. The location within the store is also important. First Interstate Bank of Texas has locations between the checkout stand and the exit, with a 45-foot banner bearing the bank's name.

The idea of supermarket banks is not universally embraced. One CEO said their customers were not used to "that much one-stop shopping." According to Chip Carlisle, Executive Vice President of First Interstate of Texas, much depends on the kind of store the branch is in.

Kay Robinson is one of the few in this survey that emphasized working with shareholders. Think of the potential of having 100 or 500 or more potential stockholder salespeople out in the community. They could also be asked for comments and suggestions, and especially for referrals. There is a big potential advantage for the bank whose stockholders are at hand and see (and like) the effect of the bank in the community.

How great it is to have marketing "pervade the institution." If employees have been brought up without concern for the customer, it takes a long time to get to where providing the best possible service is part of the atmosphere. The customer or prospect can sense that the moment he walks in and will remember it.

28

Ann H. Hawkins

Vice President, Marketing
State Bank & Trust Company
Brookhaven, MI

A newcomer program still works, but it must be worked. Ann's bank offers something of value to the newcomer. Thus, they can get information about those who are moving in before they have made bank connections.

" We have a program for newcomers that we call the 'Good Friend Program.' We began this in 1981. We have here (in Brookhaven) a General Motors plant, a Wal-Mart Distribution Center which employs many of their management people, a paper mill, and an important medical community. A packet on our bank is available through realtors and by mail. The personnel departments of the companies love us. Success in all of this requires frequent contact and convincing them that we will do a good job of serving their customer or employee.

" We offer tours for the newcomers. For example, if the hospital gives us the name of a new doctor, we may take him and his wife on a tour of a residential area, point out recreational opportunities, and talk about the history of the community. If we can sell them on our community . . . they feel that we are their friends and want us to be their banker."

29

William R. Craig

Senior Vice President
Sovran Bank, N.A.
Richmond, VA

Peter Drucker, our best known business management consultant, says our employees do not think they are on the team. Often that is true. And not just in banking. This attitude can be changed by management that emphasizes the importance of their employees. Productivity can soar as a result.

❝ At First and Merchant's National Bank (which merged with Virginia National to form Sovran) our slogan was, 'Being the best is a lifetime job.' To illustrate this we used Bobby Dandridge, a Virginian and graduate of Norfolk State, who was MVP in the National Basketball Association, and Roy Clark of country music fame, who is a native of Virginia. We also used a picture of Secretariat, the great race horse, bred in Virginia.

❝ The unexpected value of 'being the best' came when our 13,000 employees embraced this idea by striving for quality of service. This was brought out in training sessions. 'If we are going to be the best we must do so and so.'

Employees were proud to represent the bank and worked to be the best performers. They supported the promise.

Pride in being the best has been the forte of the Marine Corps and sources of strength for athletic programs with great traditions. Can't we use some of this in our business?

"Training programs talked about the importance of every individual and his or her contribution to the company. We had our slogan ('Being the best is a lifetime job') on buttons, jackets, and sports caps. Even my pastor asked for a note pad with the wording on it to use in special communications to his parishioners."

Sovran is a $22.5 billion institution with 13,000 employees and 450 branches in Virginia, Maryland, Tennessee, and the District of Columbia. Employees can identify with the slogan of a very big institution if their part is recognized.

30

Charles J. Ferrero

Senior Vice President
Midlantic Banks
Edison, NJ

Building on what we have, making one sale lead to another, and designing services that fit what we have. These are keys to profitable marketing in banking or any other endeavor.

" We have adopted a concept frequently used in the packaged goods industry. I call it 'product extension.' Our money market savings account product had plateaued and was in a down cycle. At the same time, interest rates were declining. One option to revitalize the product would have been to pay a higher rate, but we have $1.3 billion in those accounts in New Jersey and doing that would just increase the cost of funds for these deposits, without much opportunity to attract new money.

" So we designed a similar, but new product, which pays a higher rate at $25,000 and $50,000. In essence, we extended the life of the product, which is product extension. If we did not cannibalize more than 15 percent from the old product, it would be a profitable endeavor.

"We are known as the 'hungry bankers' so we named this product the 'Hungry Savers Fund.' We guaranteed the depositor that we would pay a (fluctuating) rate related to a well-known index of money market funds. We marketed this account by direct mail to the affluent market and by highly targeted newspaper advertising. We launched this and after seven months had $450 million, building at the rate of $30 million a week. The average account balances range from $95,000 to $110,000.

"Product extension can also apply to other services. For example, we currently offer a home equity loan product which is priced at 2 percent over the prime. We are looking at a new product charging 1 over the prime, but on loans of different size and different credit criteria. Again, we will use highly targeted marketing so as not to cannabilize our original home equity product line.

"Actually, we all did this same kind of thing 10 or 15 years ago. For example, when rates were raised on passbook savings accounts, banks introduced 'statement savings' and offered the higher rate only on that product, rather than increasing the rate on all regular passbook accounts."

Mr. Ferrero's bank is a $20 billion dollar institution with 440 offices in New Jersey and eastern Pennsylvania. The bank was started in 1804 and has served its customers through wars and depressions and panics. In 1989, the return on assets was running 1.2 and return on equity was 18 percent. Some record!

31

Len Huck

President (Retired)
Valley National Bank of Arizona & Valley National Corporation
Phoenix, AZ

Len believes in having marketing goals, keeping records, monitoring progress compared to goals, and rewarding performance.

      We do not yet face todays' competitive atmosphere with the kind of marketing 'culture' that we need. But the people who face the shareholders and the analysts know that *marketing is not just a sales campaign, but the way we live our daily lives as marketers.*

"There has been a noticable change in attitudes in the last five to seven years. There is more planning of where the bank wants to be. We are broadening marketing from being effective advertisers and public relations people to the more substantitive issues of reaching the bank's objectives. Another change is the insistence of management that marketing be focused on profitable products. *We are asking more efficiency and effectiveness in marketing.*

Most banking *is* a retail business. Successful marketers are proud to act like it.

"We are all retailers. We must have traffic to cross-sell. ATMs are just an option where we can give 24 hour service that can't be given in our lobbies.

"Directors should be a terrific resource in a bank's marketing program, but generally are not."

Len was one of the few CEOs of a great banking organization who came up through marketing. He has sold bank services not only as a marketer, but as a CEO responsible for overcoming all the costs and hazards of banking.

Every owner of a small business knows what Len is talking about on marketing efficiency. Sales expenses must produce profitable sales. We have had the luxury in banking of making sales calls and having fun. But now our marketing efforts have to produce results.

Why are directors generally not the "terrific resource" they should be? For a lot of reasons. A Dallas director, Ben Harris, said: "Directors must feel they are an important part of the organization." An Indiana director who sells his bank service enthusiastically explains, "I like what we are doing."

32

Mark Bodi

Senior Vice President, Retail Banking
Numerica Savings Bank
Manchester, NH

Wichita Falls, Texas, has a cycling event called "Hotter 'n Hell 100," a 100 mile bike race in heat over 100 degrees. This year 12,000 cyclists came from many states. This makes Mark's point about interest in all kinds of sports events.

❝ We have an event marketing department to maximize the marketing opportunity associated with sponsoring events. We had changed our name about four years ago and wanted to develop a positioning theme, 'Share of Mind, Share of Market.' So what was our image?

❝I was exercising one day, looking at a T-shirt, and realized that many companies had been recognized in connection with athletic events for years, but none of the financial institutions were involved in event marketing.

❝It began with athletic events, then we sponsored the Boston Pops Orchestra. People who

115

attended these events were put on our data base, and we communicated with them by mail. This was before John Hancock sponsored the Boston Marathon. Our program includes many health events.

BancFlorida in Naples has put out credit cards with pictures of the endangered Florida Panther and the Great Blue Heron, as well as participating with the state to reintroduce snook and redfish in area estuaries. Years ago I ran a bank in Dallas that made loans to restore historical old houses. Many people came in to say, "I like what you are doing and want to do business with you."

" When asked on surveys what banks were active in sponsoring athletic and community affairs, 40 percent of our customers and 25 percent of the non-customers named us. This was far better than our competition.

" We sponsored jazz and rock concerts and basketball clinics, and also looked for smaller events. For example, we print (on our own press) bookmarks for libraries and also golf cards. We get this free visibility. When Numerica Savings Bank sponsors a road race our name is on the runner's bib and when he crosses the finish line, our name stands out. We have been able to make it memorable in less than four years. The vast majority think of us as innovative and progressive.

" Our bank has a history of innovation. We were the first to offer teller machines in New Hampshire; the first to offer equity loans; the first in New England to offer a full service brokerage. Event marketing is dramatically less expensive than other kinds. For example, a TV commercial would cost $50,000 to produce and we can do a tremendous amount of good in events for that."

Mr. Bodi's bank is a $900 million institution with a dozen branches doing business throughout the southeast portion of New Hampshire.

Forty to 50 percent of most banks' non-interest expense is people related. The most successful banks use their people resources to the utmost in selling. This goes from the security guards to the board of directors. Directors? Yes. And I have yet to see a director turn down a prize for success in a sales campaign.

Customers like a bank with "firsts" to its credit. We must have more creative people in banking, like those at Numerica Savings Bank, yet we must also be able to separate the good ideas from the bad. If you do not have idea people, get some. The board is a place to start.

33

Gloria "Bunny" Able

Senior Vice President
Commerce Bank
Virginia Beach, VA

❝ One of our best marketing ideas was our 'Bahama Bash' program. Our bank was small and under new management. We were at $27 million in total resources.

❝In 1984 we carried on a program that said the first branch that gains $1 million will receive a trip to the Bahamas for all employees. We visited the branches and put on a skit, but we did not have advertising or direct mail. The new business was developed by prospecting and customer referrals. The first bank that gained a million got the trip to the Bahamas, the second got a trip to New York, and the third to a North Carolina beach. Our employees were excited and proud and this made us better salespeople. *We received over $5 million in new deposits and 90 percent stayed with us.* We did the same thing another year with a different theme.

"Employees in the operations center were told that anyone who made referrals that resulted in new business exceeding $25,000 would get to go with the winning team. However, participation was low and only one qualified.

"We are in six cities and preserve the hometown image by having a regional president in each city and give each 'presidential service' which is a new theme. We also have directors in each city. We ask directors to 'open the door' to prospective customers. We have a director's luncheon program which tells the story of Commerce Bank by an audio/visual slide presentation using testimonials from customers, directors, and employees in the slides. Directors are asked to give us two prospects who are then invited to the luncheon, introduced by the director, and *we follow up*.

"Doctors on our board have recommended how we can better serve the medical community and if a director wants to invite 10 new doctors to see the 'Med Advantage' program, we appreciate and encourage it. We have developed a package of services not only for the doctor, but the (doctor's) office staff as well."

Commerce Bank is an exception to the general truth expressed by Len Huck when he said, "Directors should be a terrific resource (in marketing), but generally they are not."

> **Having a regional president and directors in each city says, "This *is* a large institution but with local roots. We care about this community." Having the door to prospects opened by directors greatly increases the percentage of sales from calls. And do not pass by the idea of directors' luncheons. It has so many pluses. Yet, in all my interview calls, almost no bankers mentioned directors as a marketing resource, and nobody mentioned directors' spouses!**

The bank of which I was CEO once had an opthamologist on the board. He started enthusiastically. Later he said, "I'm going to resign. I'm not contributing." I had to say, "You're right, but it is my fault." Why didn't I ask him how we could better serve the medical community? It is the responsibility of the Chairman and the CEO to make it possible for every director to contribute. Then, if the director chooses not to contribute, he should ask himself, "Shouldn't I resign so someone else can use this position?"

Some directors can contribute in one way and some in another. It is their collective experience, judgment, and contacts that makes the board valuable.

34

Dana Dowd Williams

Senior Vice President
First Fidelity Bank Corp.
Newark, NJ

❝❝ In 1987 our bank was 175 years old. *We have paid uninterrupted dividends since 1812.* To recognize this we put on nine free concerts, attended by 110,000 people. This was done by the New Jersey Pops Orchestra in conjunction with the New Jersey Park System. Each concert concluded with Tchaikovsky's '1812 Overture' and the fireworks, which are called for by a certain section of the Overture.

❝ On July fourth we did a concert before the Statue of Liberty which was carried by CNN. For all those occasions we had outstanding recognition from the press. The whole program was announced by the Governor and our Chairman, from the Governor's office.

Benefits of some of the more productive marketing ideas are indirect and hard to measure. But they are what people talk about and what they weigh in evaluating a possible bank connection. Many relate to fundamentals as old as banking itself—quality, strength, stability, and service to customers and community. What better thing could a bank say than, "We've been here since 1812 through war, panic, and depression, and we'll be here when you need us in the future."

"We continued our leadership in the arts with three concerts in 1988, attended by a total of 60,000 people of the kind we would like to have as customers. One of the concerts was in Newark and drew the largest audience there in more than 25 years."

The First Fidelity Bank Corporation is a $30 billion organization in New Jersey and Pennsylvania which showed leadership of the kind that people admire. What this bank is doing speaks to quality, to history, to durability, and to strength. These are the things banking has been about since its beginning.

Obviously, money was spent on this. But this bank was born about the time the British were burning the White House and Francis Scott Key wrote the "Star Spangled Banner." They will not add another 175 years to this record of service until A.D. 2162. Such an occasion can be suitably celebrated only by a powerful, lasting, and high quality idea.

35

Jim Volk

President
United New Mexico Bank of Las Cruces
Las Cruces, NM

Chip Carlisle, Executive Vice President, First Interstate Bank of Texas, said they selected Randall's Food Markets for their branches because of Randall's reputation for service and outstanding growth. These branches are open 9:00 to 7:00 every day of the week. Banks and other financial institutions have a major potential for displaying their services in the bank lobby. Many did better on this 30 years ago.

" We put a branch in a supermarket in 350 square feet. It is right inside the door with a new accounts person, consumer lender, and a teller's window.

"One of these grocery store branches can be put in for about $130,000 compared to a half-million for the traditional branch. We must have the right kind of person working there; someone who likes action and noise.

"We learned a lot about marketing from this experience. When we put in displays we found that they were not as attractive as those being used by the grocery store. We have also had a hard time convincing people that we actually

What kind of loans do you make and do your customers know?

make loans there. So we put a big picture of the lender pointing his finger (just like Uncle Sam) saying, 'See me for a loan.' We also do premium things there, like in the (old) silverware days.

"Saturday mornings we might have a clown helping with a birthday party and registering people for a trip. Many of our officers are around there just shaking hands. We have 20,000 people coming past this grocery store bank.

"Our main bank is in an upper-income area and there we sponsor what we call a 'classic' account for retirees which has special benefits. The average balances would have entitled these customers to the benefits anyway. The walkers club was an offshoot from that and we called it a 'classic walkers club.' The bank furnishes coffee and we keep records of the mileage. Once a month the hospital is there to take blood pressure.

J. B. Wheeler, President, Hale County State Bank, Plainview, Texas, and former President of the Texas Bankers Association, says "The best marketing idea I've ever had in all my years in banking is to lead in civic improvement for the growth of the town."

"When we opened our bank four years ago, we wanted to identify with the community. We would spend $10,000 for an opening, so instead of that we said to the community, 'We have $10,000 to give to your favorite United Way charity, $1,000 to each of the top ten.' Then we went to the United Way organizations and said: 'You can get $1,000 by asking your supporters to come to our bank and vote for you.' Poeple who give to charities have money. We got a fine mailing list and had two weeks in which to do it. In the usual opening you have only one day and do not have time to do anything."

Jim Volk is a part of the United New Mexico holding company and is in a rapidly growing area. Creativity is evident in his marketing ideas. Banking needs to attract and reward creative people. He is right about the usual bank opening. His plan is better.

36

Larry Ness

President/CEO
First Dakota National Bank
Yankton, SD

If your bank is in an area with many people 55 or over, consider organizing a group that appeals especially to them. The bank needs what these groups have. Banks can provide social and intellectual activity to the organizations. Members invite their friends. Among the members in the Emerald Club at our own bank, there have been two weddings! No wonder it sells itself.

❝ One of our best ideas has been the formulation of a travel club of senior citizens. They pay $5.00 to join. There are about 160 members and they are quite loyal to the bank. At their meetings they talk about where they would like to go and then come to a decision. The farthest they have gone is a cruise to Hawaii.

❝ We are in an agricultural area and our farm department developed a trip to Las Vegas to the National Rodeo Finals. We chartered a plane and it sold out.

❝ We give a "high test" customer appreciation dinner with a floor show, and are the only ones doing it in this area. Also there are small lunches in our board room with about ten customers and two of our officers.

"Customers furnish the program by talking about their businesses. We have customers call asking to be invited.

"Yankton is a historic city of about 12,000 people. We were the last steamboat stop on the Missouri River, so settlers came through here, including such famous expeditions as Lewis and Clark. We were the first bank organized in the Dakota territories and the steamships kept their accounts with us."

If you do not make your history known, your long, quality service, in good times and bad, may be forgotten by the customer, especially when he has a complaint.

Larry's bank, which was chartered in 1872, has earned more than 1.5 percent on assets for each of the last five years and 1.88 percent most recently. It is now a $130 million organization. Continued progress with a combination of old and new is inspiring. They earned money in troubled times and kept on serving the agricultural customer.

37

Joyce Healey

Senior Vice President
Manufacturers Hanover Trust Company
New York, NY

▟▟ In retail banking, marketing is a lot closer to that of Pepsico than what has been traditional in our industry. We must involve the four P's:

Product, Price, Place, Promotion.

" In a deregulated world, marketing must be closely involved with product. Should your IRA accounts offer mutual funds? Should you have a money market fund for small businesses? We do, and it's a parking place for money the business does not need at the moment. It's a different product with a different rate than other money market accounts and carries analysis fees.

One banker who conducted a survey said it showed they have customers who "hate" going to the bank. Just think of one of the ten largest departments in the bank functioning entirely by mail and telephone. This is not just loan by phone, but all-around banking.

"The price on our liabilities is managed by my (marketing department) product managers. For example, they attend the asset/liability committee meetings. Sometimes we want a wider interest spread. Sometimes we are content with a narrow spread, or may even be willing to accept a negative spread for particular reasons. This involves alternative forms of distribution. One of our branches functions by mail and over the telephone and is one of the ten largest in the organization.

"Promotion. This is marketing developed around our product managers. They must go to those who perform the service and others who will sell the service as a part of designing both product and promotion. They are 'middle men.' A lot of understanding and negotiation is required. This process includes consumer credit, but business credit is handled by the lenders.

I have read that Toyota gets nearly one idea per week per employee and uses most of them. In many banks people with ideas do not advance them because they are afraid of making waves. A lot of trust must be developed to get the upward communication which is so valuable because it comes from where the action is. It enables us to seize opportunities and to stop problems before they get big.

"*Ideas can come from anywhere*. Branch managers have a part of a common marketing budget and also their own budget to be used, for example, if the local schools want some assistance from us.

"Our (marketing) product managers cover five sectors: international, corporate, investment, retail, and asset-based lending. They are among the senior people who have to go out and work in the branches in order to maintain their function. Frequently this results in redesign of a product or the creation of a new one."

In many cases "big bankers" never get the feel of the local market or what is going on in the local bank or branch. The heads of manufacturing or retail companies spend much time in their plants and stores. Many factory executives have their offices on the factory floor. Recent banking problems suggest some bankers do not know enough about what is going on. We must have honest and timely input from boards, officers, and employees. My secretary once prevented a big problem by notifying me of things she had observed about a large customer.

Much thought should be given to local charitable contributions. People still start every drive with the bank. Bank participation is expected, yet banks cannot afford to give to everything, or in the amounts asked. Some banks concentrate on making a real impact in certain vital areas, for example, local schools.

38

Kim Albert

Vice President, Retail Banking
First American Bank
Minot, ND

Mr. Albert's description of planning and the promising gains resulting from it is the best I have seen. This must all take place within the overall objectives of the institution. Planning should flow up, and sideways, as well as down. The best way to get employees to feel they are on the team is to let them help shape the future.

" Every year when we develop our strategic plan, we set goals, and at the end of all the planning, we tell our employees what we want to accomplish. But previously we had not told them what their part was.

" Now, when we develop our plan, we begin with a sales plan *and every person sets goals.* The goals of the retail bankers are rolled up into the department goals. The goals of all the lending departments become the lending goals for the bank. *Each loan officer has a job description which incorporates not only sales goals, but quality. This is measured by charge-offs, classified loans, non-performing loans, and past dues.*

"Our PIE program stands for pride in excellence. For example, new accounts will get six pieces of pie every month for performance in six different categories, such as cross-sell ratio, number of sales, and so forth. One employee might get all of those or none. An employee who gets six pieces of pie can redeem them for cash, time off, or other recognition.

"We are now working on other types of incentives for bookkeepers and secretaries. *We had some grumbling when we started this program, but, for example, credit life on loans has increased by 400 percent and the impact on the bottom line quickly overcomes this opposition.* Now when we announce our objectives for the new year, every person knows his part, and feels that if he can accomplish this, the bank can reach its goals."

A bank that has all its customer contact people reporting to someone who has no interest in selling will always be fighting an uphill battle in marketing.

First American is a $120 million bank. All the loan departments (except commercial) plus new accounts and tellers report to Mr. Albert. This organizational structure emphasizes marketing. Bank officers and employees often express that they do not know what the bank is trying to do or their part in it. If board and top executives can get agreement on the banks' objectives, they will naturally break down to departments, and within the departments to individuals. A bank that has that will not have to worry about the competition. However, most have made very little progress in this direction.

Many of the loan problems in banks and savings and loans would not have developed if officers' job descriptions had been thoughtful and balanced, emphasizing quality as well as volume. It would have been apparent when they could not make the volume quotas and keep up quality standards. A choice would have been faced. At least this conflict would have generated discussion. Kim Albert's program has to do with much more than marketing.

39

Alex MacFadyen

General Vice President, Director of Corporate Communications
First Citizens Bank
Raleigh, NC

Well-organized, short-term promotions with measured results and reward for production can pay off in a big way. But they are only part of a broad, long-term marketing effort that involves the whole organization.

❝ Special product emphasis through employee incentives has been very productive. We take a specific product and boost it for ninety days. For example, the home equity loans. We had been on it a year and interest was lagging. *We put on a ninety day promotion. For every equity line the employee solicited which was put on the books*, we paid $50.00. Half-way in the program that was increased to $100.00. The employee handed out the application with his or her name on it and this qualified them for the bonus. We did not reduce our credit standards.

❝The average of these lines was $30,000 and in a 90 day period, we more than doubled the total credit lines by doubling the number of accounts. There was skepticism that the new lines would not be used. But the percentage outstanding is the same now as it was before the program so the customers did use them."

First Citizens Bank is a $3 billion institution with 300 branches still staying close to its customers and doing creative things to develop business and reward employees.

40

Kim Ouren

Marketing Officer
Dakota Bank
Fargo, ND

Some banks have arranged to be shopped on how the telephone is answered, or how calls are returned, or how customers are greeted in the lobby, and have learned much about their services. These customer comments should go to the highest executive level. As CEO, I was sometimes surprised at adverse customer reactions that seemed unjustified—but the customer *is* right—whether he is correct or not.

66 Our shopper programs have made a noticeable improvement in our customer service. We use our own customers as shoppers. The shoppers make two visits a month, and every four weeks we change. They are now shopping the tellers. We will also do the lenders. Those who are shopped can earn points (in several categories) if they do well and that is combined monthly and quarterly for money incentives.

" In selecting the shoppers we'd like one to be a business person, one a consumer, and one retired. They have a nice lunch with the president in which all get better acquainted and we pay $10.00 for each report. We have had cus-

One of the objectives of shopping should be to spot outstanding service. The officers and employees should know it is being done and why—it is not spying. Recently, I called a big Dallas bank to see if they had somebody in the executive and professional department who would like to present the bank's financing program to new doctors. The secretary I got just kept going until she found the right person. I felt that a bank with employees like this must be good.

tomers comment that our service has noticeably improved.

The CEO should not fail to have his own office shopped to see what barriers have been set up there.

Dakota Bank and Trust has $125 million in assets with three locations in Fargo. They not only emphasize service, but have an effective way of determining if they are giving it.

I have been on the receiving end of some great service that changed my attitude about the whole organization. I hope the persons who gave it were recognized and rewarded. One of the areas that can make the biggest difference is secretarial.

41

Kurt Watson

Executive Vice President
Bank IV
Wichita, KA

The marketing culture must start with the chief executive or people will not believe in it. If the chief thinks selling is beneath him, or is just the concern of the marketing department, nobody will want to be a part of that. The team will gravitate to "where the real bankers are" and the damage to the bank's position and customer base may never be repaired.

❝ Bank IV Wichita has built its success on a commitment to "asking for the business." This commitment began in the 1940s when then Chairman A. W. Kincaid stated, "If something is going to happen in Wichita, Bank IV will be right in the middle of it." As a result, Bank IV Wichita is the state's largest bank and enjoys a 40 percent market share in a city of 282,000 people in a Standard Metropolitan Statistical Area of 400,000.

❝ Running a six week sales training program followed by a business development effort that lasts for a few weeks will not make your organization marketing-driven. *Being marketing-driven is something that takes years to develop.*

An organization must commit itself and then live up to that commitment every day. A marketing culture must start at the very top of any organization. The best marketing guy in the country working for a CEO who does not think marketing is important will be frustrated and unsuccessful.

" Being marketing-driven means very simply that everything you do is targeted at serving the customer. The customer is the single most important person in any organization and finding a way to enhance that customer relationship and create new customers is the only reason for us to be in business.

" Our marketing organization is structured to include two departments whose sole responsibility is the retention and acquisition of business.

" One department, Commercial Business Development, serves our business banking customers. Each commercial account has an assigned business development representative, and this representative is the "relationship manager" of the account. If the customer has a need, from leasing equipment to ordering new checks, this person is there to see that it happens quickly and efficiently. These people also make calls on prospective customers, and their compensation and advancement are dependent upon their success.

" The second department, Private Banking, was established for our best retail banking customers. If the relationship concept worked so well on the commercial side of the bank why wouldn't it prove equally successful for our outstanding personal banking customers?

Years ago my wife had an obscure disease, and we finally took her to the great Mayo Clinic. There were several doctors involved, but there was a "head doctor" who made the final diagnosis and prescribed successful treatment. Years ago the "head financial doctor" in a bank was probably the CEO. Now, it is more complicated and needs special attention and cooperation. Our customer needs one banker he can call on. If it is necessary to refer the customer, he or she should still feel he has a "head banker" responsible for the whole relationship. Balance the load. If top executives get bogged down in this, they cannot manage.

"The concept here is the same. We have private bankers, each with their own portfolio of present customers; and each private banker is expected to solicit new business through an ongoing calling program. Both departments have proved to be extremely successful for one reason. We are providing our customers with what they deserve—outstanding personal service and attention. *No new product or marketing program could ever manage the success that we have achieved by simply serving our best customers to the fullest extent.*

If we get and keep the top customers, we have those most likely to grow and least likely to cause trouble or loss. This provides a built-in growth from customers we know and trust.

"Obviously, in a large banking institution, this type of personal service can't be provided for everyone. Ten percent of our customers provide 90 percent of our deposits. It is our singular goal that this 10 percent receive outstanding service. The resulting effect is that the other 90 percent of our customers benefit from this commitment. We need only to remind ourselves that the customer is 'king,' and if we do that we cannot help but grow and continue to be successful and profitable.

"I believe strongly that everyone must be committed to selling. This includes our operations people. *Remember, selling is merely dedication to customer service,* and everyone throughout our organization must be committed to that.

Providing marketing support for each bank (or branch) in its own community has been good to many institutions. Regardless of what they see on television, people believe the performance they experience.

"All this has a "trickle down" effect. We now have people throughout the bank asking for the business because of this sales culture.

"Each of the banks in this holding company is a separate entity and carries on its own marketing program. If the bank in Coffeyville needs to buy the prize steer at the fair they can do it, although that would not be important in Wichita."

In Texas, nearly all the bank holding companies were formed at the same time and were running the same race. Eight of the largest ten were merged or failed. In writing *The Dynamic Financial Manager* I talked to executives and directors of three of the failed institutions. Each mentioned that more input and diversity could have been retained had more power and flexibility been left in the local institutions.

42

William G. Price

Chairman and CEO
First Bank of Immokalee
Immokalee, FL

And any bank can provide a prompt response to loan requests. It is not a sign of sophisticated lending when customers have to wait three weeks for an answer on routine loans. It is a sign of indecisive and, probably, disorganized lending!

❝ We try to give the best service we can as quickly as we can with a "can do" and never a "can't do" attitude. We stay involved in the community and respond happily, not grudgingly, to the community institution.

❝*The majority of our loan customers get the money on their first trip to the bank. For major lines of credit, which require board approval, we anticipate their needs and get approval in advance.* We try to beat the competition with instant, better, and more personal service. We believe we make loans to people and not to things.

The banker who is hard to get on the telephone is saying, "I'm too busy to work with you." The customer can find one who is not.

" Every person is important enough for me to talk to. We don't screen the calls. If somebody wants to talk to the Chairman of the Board they get to talk to the Chairman of the Board. If a call comes in for me and I'm busy, the operator will have that call on my desk in 60 seconds so I can give a quick response."

Mr. Price's bank is $20 million in total assets in a farming comunity with a population of 14,000 people. He expects to make two percent on assets this year. His average is 1.6 for the last five years.

The effectiveness of a committee system depends on its members, what they are asked to do, and the CEOs way of dealing with them. An agricultural bank in Georgia made great use of committees, including directors, in evaluating agricultural loans. However, it is a mistake to think that a loan is good just because it went through the directors' loan committee. The worst loan we ever made went through the directors' committee not once, but twice.

The "can do" attitude will be sensed and appreciated by the customer. Even if the bank must say "no," the customer will know we tried.

In the early years of my banking career, in a small bank, nearly all the qualified customers got the money on the first trip to the bank. No one thought of doing otherwise. But the old-time bankers went over every new loan the next morning. Between them they knew what was going on in the community and with the customers. This meant fast service for the customer and safety for the bank. Many banks, even some large ones, still rely on good loan officers and effective after-the fact review. But meanwhile, committees became bigger and slower and dominated the lending process. They, in turn, were often dominated by a few members. Speed of service was lost and diversity of input was often reduced. Every bank should look at its credit granting process and ask, "Does this really get the right answers and in a timely way?"

One very large and highly successful Pacific Coast bank allows considerable freedom for the loan officer (within loan limits), but the department head and others participate in an effective after-the-fact review which can bring about changes before more damage is done. If this group sees weaknesses in the loan, the officer will move to cure them.

First Bank of Immokalee was chartered in 1923 in Everglades City, Florida, and was moved to Immokalee in 1962. The growth has been steady, with the bank now about 12 times the size it was when it moved to the present location.

43

Fred Shenk, Jr.

Senior Vice President
First National Bank of Glens Falls
Glens Falls, NY

Fred's bank illustrates that incentive programs can permit everyone to participate in some way and win recognition. This proves to people who are not sales-oriented that selling can be fun, and they can do it. Much of selling financial services is knowing the business and giving good service with enthusiasm. Fred says, "Initially we wanted everyone to win and minimum standards were set low. We have been able to move these standards up."

❝ The best thing that has happened here is described by an often overused term 'sales culture.' We have been able to do that because of the sales attitude of our CEO. This is most important.

❝ We work also on commission payments and incentives. If a person in new accounts sells three services to a new customer who comes in to open a checking account, they receive four dollars. The tellers who go so long without being out of balance are also recognized with a gold name plate, dinner with the president, and a check for $1,000. Proof operators are recognized for a number of items and limited number of mistakes.

Increasing the number of products sold per interview is a great achievement. Any bank that concentrates on that can do it.

" *Before we began this program we had a sale ratio of 1.5 products per interview. Now it is more than three products per interview. That helps us keep the customer, which is the most important thing in marketing.*

" Much training is involved. *Our people must know how to help the customer find his real needs.* There are some areas where it is difficult to put a dollar value on a particular service. However, everyone can participate in the bank-wide program and achievements and be recognized by attending a banquet for all who perform above a certain level. There we give awards and money too.

" In all this we are creating the conviction that 'we are here to serve the customer.' Every month our CEO meets with all the staff people in small groups and gets their feedback. They make suggestions, every one of which is evaluated, and the employee receives a letter telling him what has been done, or if nothing, why. *They feel they have the freedom to speak up and we get their input.* Our bank has 50 employees and 90 percent of them own stock.

Many more banks are putting training under marketing to foster this "sales culture." This means the marketers must really know banking, probably from previous banking experience. That will also make them more outstanding marketers. The marketers are at the real heartbeat of the bank. The object is not to have the "marketers" and the "others," but one team working together for a common goal.

" *In our bank, training falls under marketing rather than personnel because we are anxious to get the sales culture into that training.*"

I would like to repeat one statement from Mr. Shenk. "Our people must help the customer find his real needs." The business consultant with the best sales record I know says he tries not to say anything but to ask questions for the first 30 minutes of a sales call. He is trying to get the customer to express his needs and then develop plans to meet at least some of them. In many sales calls, I have heard the banker talking a lot about his bank. But time after time good marketers have said their customers do not see a big distinction between banks. We need to get the prospects to talk about their needs and tell the client how much of that we can meet.

Upward communication is one of the most valuable assets a bank can have. I can think of many cases where upward communication could have saved millions. But as one banker said, "somebody must be listening."

"This is *my* bank and this job is my business." If an employee gets that attitude, productivity can leap and the possibility of costly turnover goes down.

I can sympathize with the good systems person who wants to avoid sales. When I first entered banking years ago I was assigned to post the old Boston style general ledger with pen and ink. My accounting apptitude is .02. I had to walk around the block every morning to get nerve enough to go in and face what was for me a very dreary job. I was grateful to move to the lending area where I had good support and I knew I could do the job.

Fred's bank is in the area made famous by James Fenimore Cooper's novel, *The Last of the Mohicans*. There are two local banks in the community and five years ago First National was $100 million larger than the competition. Now it is $200 million larger. This bank is now a $550 million institution and part of a $700 million holding company. *They emphasize that creative commercial lenders with low loan losses make a great contribution to growth and fine profits.* Fred's bank shows that loan officers can be strongly positive and creative in serving the customer and still have low loan losses if they are good enough.

This bank occasionally transfers an employee to another area if they do not feel like they want to participate in the sales program, but do not fire them. Some employees just cannot accept a marketing culture. All of us are a lot more comfortable in the areas of our main talents and interest.

44

Ben Meek

President and CEO
Kaw Valley State Bank
Wamego, KS

66 We have donated a message board assigned to our Chamber of Commerce. It carries our name and looks like our sign, but the Chamber is responsible for getting an outstanding location, for maintaining it, and selecting the message. The sign is programmable. For example, there is a local festival. Also, we are a 'main street city,' which refers to the federal program that helps bring in outside experts with recommendations on how to improve our city. The message board fits right into that new thrust.

"We are in a slow growing area, but support efforts exist to keep our community, and especially the downtown area, from deteriorating. Our bank is playing an important part.

" Our slogan is 'the bank of personal service.' We note any milestone in the families or businesses of our customers. We recognize the births of children by sending a plate inscribed with the name and date of birth and weight of the child. Later, we send cards and, eventually, the child is invited to the annual party for high school seniors. Cards are also used to recognize wedding anniversaries and we give plates for the 25th and 50th. We pay special attention to our customers who are in the hospital. Family bibles that are sent to the customer's children who are getting married are important. When anyone's picture or activities are in the paper we send a copy of the laminated article.

" Most of our business comes from a 10 mile radius. However, we are close to a couple of larger cities and we can penetrate those markets with home mortgage lending. We convince the realtors that if anyone can get the loan approved, we can. These loans are sold into the secondary market and we make the origination fee."

One banker in a town of 1,500 asks, "Will this town even be here in 10 years?" This question is an important one that should get the attention of most small town bankers. The follow-up question to this is, "What can this bank do to see that it is?" While some small towns are deteriorating, others are stable or growing. Leadership is the difference and often this starts with the bankers.

Ben's bank is a 75 year old, $30 million institution, in a town of 4,000 people competing with another bank and two savings and loan associations. This community has the same problems that face so many others, continuing deterioration of the downtown. The bank can be a strong force in building the community and, in doing so, preserve its own market. The creativity of Kaw Valley State Bank benefitted the town of Wamego and also provided a continuing advertising source for a low, one-time cost.

Sometimes there is a temptation to give up on community improvements when residential deterioration spreads, business buildings are vacant, and there is an influx of pawn shops and bars as established businesses move out. But it is surprising what can happen from small beginnings. Many have started with beautification, perhaps street plantings, spreading to improved store fronts and interiors. However, for a community to really improve, the residential area must also look up. And it doesn't have to be with large and expensive homes. Old rundown sections have shown marked improvement when people see improvement and believe it will continue.

Banks have been leaders and strong participants in most of these programs.

45

Diane Pearce

Vice President
West One Bank
Boise, ID

▟▟ Our best marketing idea was to know our market, with the realization that each market is different. We are in Northwest Utah, Idaho, Oregon, and Washington. The high-growth area in Washington is different than the other areas that we serve, which are primarily agricultural.

"We used all the marketing techniques, including surveys of our own as well as those that we purchased on contract. *Our local bank managements and state boards of directors have been an important influence in developing this information.*

159

"But the second part of this is even more important, and often neglected. *We must make a self-analysis.* Who are we, what resources do we have now, and what are we likely to have in the future? *We are more likely to fail in analyzing our own internal capabilities than in the study of the market.* We must organize all the information that we have and use all of our resources, including boards and local management."

Diane is 100 percent right about the neglect of candid self-analysis. It often becomes self-deceit. Bankers tend to think we are smarter than others, especially if our banks are bigger. That leads to thinking that none of the bad things we hear about will happen to us. I have participated in more than four dozen "retreats" with individual banks and their boards, which focus mainly on planning. Analyzing the banks' strengths and weaknesses is a usual part of the process. It is very hard to honestly answer the question, "Where are we weak?" But let us not start by saying, "We are strong in management and in the board," when the opposite may be true and needs to be recognized. A candid but positive approach is to ask, "Where is improvement needed?"

When I have the opportunity to talk to bankers over the country, I am often asked, "Why didn't your lenders in Texas recognize the dangerous overbuilding in real estate that was occurring?" Bankers in other states are now asking themselves that same question. More than one outstanding real estate lender has pointed out that he or she continued to analyze real estate loans based upon credit analysis of borrowers and contractors, appraisals and values, track records, economic justification, probable cash flows and the needs for not only that project, but other projects and much other information that would normally have been sufficient. But it was "what was going on around the project that would cause it to fail." Often that involved much more than real estate. When the oil service companies in the Southwest began to shrink, their office needs shrank too.

In many areas of the country, crime, drugs, and environmental problems have driven property values down dramatically. One good surviving CEO asked, "Is anybody reading our (Texas) book? We paid billions for it." It does not appear to have been a best seller, but many of the same symptoms are appearing in other parts of the country.

Often information comes to us in scraps. I asked one former CEO whose bank had failed, "What would you do differently if you had another chance?" He answered, "Get away and think." He added, "I had enough information about what was happening if I had put it all together."

The CEO of a $50 million bank may not plan to hire market analysts, but he does have many sources of information, especially his board, that is or should be broadly representative of every business interest in the community. One chairman says, "We should be the leading edge of information for the CEO." The office manager of a real estate firm says she drives a different route every day between home and office, noting what is happening, even how the yards are kept. Our officers and employees can do the same. We do have plenty of sources of information, but as Diane emphasizes, *we must put it all together.*

As emphasized by West One Bank, the total analysis of our market and ourselves is not as easy as many think. During the early phase of the Texas economic nose dive, I sat here invested in bank stock, thinking I knew banking, the market, and the companies involved. It turned out I knew less about all of that than I fancied. Let us really use all of the knowledge we can get about ourselves and our market, and then "get away and think."

I have participated in about 50 "retreats" where directors and their managements get away from the telephone and the secretary and ask, "What kind of bank do we want to have in three to five years and how are we going to get there?" This last is largely a marketing question. Some of these sessions have been a half day in the board room. Others have been a long weekend in Bermuda. I recommend Bermuda.

All have made a great start in planning, though many do not get the benefit of following up or of involving the people who can make the plan come true. It is good to give spouses at least the option to attend, including the meetings. Of course the CEO or any executive can also benefit by just spending a quiet weekend afternoon at the bank to "put it all together."

46

C. Paul Johnson

Chairman
First Colonial Bankshares
Chicago, IL

In most banks only a few officer calls are well prepared, well conducted, followed up, and monitored for results. Sometimes the call, rather than the result, becomes the objective.

" " Marketing is taking a whole different direction. One of our ideas is to hire salespeople and teach them banking, rather than trying to make salespeople out of bankers. We hire marketing people. The old-time call program by lending officers is inadequate. They (the officers) were centered in accounting and it's difficult for them to make a sales call.

" We have a sales office in our group of 11 banks, which includes several small ones. There are five sales people in this office, more than half of whom are attractive young women. They must and do know what we can do. When we acquire or open a bank, we assign three people from this (sales) office for approximately two months. They target the businesses in the area and write a letter to say that we would like an appointment to present a needs analysis. This letter is mailed to arrive on Tuesday. We call several days later and get an appointment in 30 percent of the cases.

"When we go back for a subsequent meeting, the salesperson frequently asks for the opportunity to bring the president, who then gets to see this place of business. When we have presented the needs analysis, we actually get some business 30 percent of the time.

"Sometimes it is good to 'cut our losses short' and terminate the calls because a lot of prospects are not interested or do not fit. We don't want to take the president out there until these prospects have been screened by $25,000 a year people who are expected to make 15 calls a week.

"We also have a very good management training program and hire six trainees a year from the outstanding universitities in this area. We put them in the sales office for three months to absorb the sales culture. They see what it is like to make calls and to get turned down. They have to be good to fit into our organization.

"One benefit of putting our salespeople in the new organization or the one we have acquired for a period of time is that they definitely make a strong impact on the sales consciousness of the whole bank."

*U*sing this approach First Colonial brought a new bank up to $10 million in four months.

Who to call on? This is one of the first questions to be answered in a good call program. This screening program covers ground, saves valuable time for both banker and prospect, and reaches the right people. The second question is, "Have I properly prepared?" Then conduct the call in a way that gets at the customers' needs. This is why the needs analysis helps, and the selling banker needs to be willing to take a bit of a beating like other salesmen. Whoever is instrumental in hiring can find out if job applicants have the personality and determination that are essential to successful selling.

This is a carefully planned and organized system, backed by training that puts in place all the elements of successful selling and still permits the day-to-day banker to mind the store. The cost/benefit ratio is bound to be better than the typical officer call programs where an officer, whose time may be costing the bank $100.00 an hour (counting all the perquisites and expenses of support costs), spends two hours over an expensive lunch making an introductory approach. Banks doing officer calling are doing well. Those who analyze actual costs against results do better.

47

David Blake

Vice President, Marketing
BankEast Corporation
Manchester, NH

❝ Our best marketing idea has been to establish a *retail sales culture*, beginning in 1984. There is nothing tougher and nothing more worthwhile.

❝ Most of the people we employed in customer contact positions were order takers. Customers had to know what they wanted when they arrived. In 1984 we began to define these contact jobs into true sales positions. This was to capitalize on lobby opportunities.

❝ We teach our tellers how to do lead development, followed by extensive work with 'platform people' on closing sales. Our account representatives typically are retail lenders, or in our investment department and spend one-third of their time on outbound telemarketing which sometimes extends beyond normal business hours.

Make a grid of your most profitable marketing opportunities. Near the top of the list will be officers talking to customers in the lobby to find and to serve additional banking needs. But it is hard to get bankers to do this. One bank has hour glasses on each officer's desk. Every 50 minutes he or she goes into the lobby for 10 minutes to meet customers. Another has a "Red Coat Banker" program. The guys and gals in the red coats are assigned to be what one calls "information specialists" for that day.

"We have in place all elements of a sales culture, including tracking and incentive compensation, which may amount to as much as 20 percent of salary. However, there is no credit for just taking the order. We expect a teller to deliver a sales message in one-half of the customer transactions. Our tellers have 315,000 customer transactions per quarter and one percent of those should translate into leads. The teller must develop leads from more than the assigned quota to receive incentive compensation.

"Central Marketing handles all the essential sales tracking. We must know who is doing what.

"Our lobby efforts result in $60 million a year in deposit business that we would not otherwise have. *It's not just the volume, but what we can do with the pricing that is most important.* We can resist the temptation to meet all the rate competition and still retain our deposit base. *Our interest margin is significantly better than the competition. This is the big payoff.*

"We do not have our commercial bankers involved. That's another animal.

"All this began in 1984 because we had become dissatisfied with the typical short-term approaches and contacted Sarah Griffin of Sales and Telemarketing Resources, Inc., a consultant in our area. We invested almost a

This is a *big* investment for a *continuing* program. We cannot expect to make operations people into salespeople in a short and easy lesson. In many cases it cannot be done at all. I can imagine how I would react if assigned to the operations center.

quarter of a billion dollars in on-site training time over two years to establish the basic sales behavior. We now have three full-time, in-house sales trainers.

" This effort is easy to give up on. It takes a lot of time. It tends to upset the apple cart. We are in a high employment area where ordinary bank-wide turnover may run over 40 percent annualized, and during the time we were installing this, we probably pushed that up more towards 60 percent. Many people had been hired without any understanding that they were going to be in a sales job, and our success has been much better with the more recent hires.

" We do not expect sales efforts from technicians. Every person must be responsible for the primary job component. If then we get a referral in addition to that, so much the better. We believe anything worth asking people to do is worth measuring, and this is essential to the success of the program."

Despite some discouraging statistics, small customers do grow. If they do not, who is expanding and branching into new endeavors? Nobody starts big.

BankEast is a $1.1 billion company with 33 offices over southern New Hampshire. Branch managers make calls directed at small business, which "commercial banking typically tends to overlook." David says this has been the least successful aspect of the program and probably only five of the 30 managers are really effective. However, they make 600 calls on businesses per quarter, and those calls would not have been made except for this effort.

The fulcrum of the whole BankEast program is *sales in the lobby*. This is where much of our opportunity is and where we can approach the customer, with whom we already have a connection, in the most efficient way to talk about additional accounts, credit cards, loans, or trust business and referrals. When you consider that this whole effort enables the bank to maintain its deposit base at a lower cost than competitors and, thus, get a premium interest margin, the benefits are tremendous.

48

William Travis

Senior Vice President
First National Bank of Toledo
Toledo, OH

❝ We market our institution as the bank of 'uncommon services' and believe that service is not just a matter of marketing, but of surviving. We now have intensified competition, especially by credit unions, which are now expanding into leasing, mortgage lending, and are serving companies other than those of their origin.

Market share, reputation, staff development, and management succession all are assets (or liabilities) of a bank—as surely as if they were on the balance sheet.

❝We must first produce the level of service and then market it as a way of differentiating between ourselves and our competitors.

❝Other banks may cut costs and continue to cut until service is marginal, *but investors looking at short-term results may not realize what is really happening.* We constantly have to sell our stockholders on the long-term values of what we are doing. Good service does cost more, but we believe people are willing to pay a bit more, as we are willing to go a little bit farther to a dry cleaner that gives us the service that we really expect.

I know of a restaurant that did great business until they began to cut the number of waitresses. Probably every new local manager got points at headquarters for this. This restaurant always had enough waitresses until the day it was closed because it no longer had enough customers to keep the doors open.

"Our research shows that there is an absolute demand, a groundswell, from the customer that says, 'We do not have to put up with poor service and we are not going to.' We tend to be like the railroads which charged each customer more, but were carrying fewer passengers, until they finally went out of the passenger business.

"Our bank spends lots of money on training and provides an abundance of internal recognition. We are emphasizing a program also to provide external recognition for our officers and employees, though we still do not have an incentive compensation program. This is working well.

"In the banking business, there are great opportunities because of a broad customer base and our operating skills. If we are going to be beaten by the competitors, it will be because we are outmarketed." Amen.

Think how much more difficult it is for a consumer credit company to book home improvement loans, for example, than for the local bank to solicit that loan from its own customer. But many such companies are growing and prospering by getting the kind of business on which local banks could have a competitive edge.

L. L. Bean, the legendary founder of the famous company that bears his name and sells outdoor equipment from the little town of Freeport, Maine, started in a shoe repair shop. He designed a new type of boot for hunters. Ninety of the first 100 pairs were returned because the soles came loose from the uppers. He could have made excuses and saved money, but he scraped up the money to refund every customer, and redesigned the boot. This company now has annual sales of over $350 million. It is, as one observer said, built on "total reliability." Similarly, one fine CEO said, "If the bank is wrong, it should correct quickly and cheerfully."

Good service does cost more. Bank stock analysts may miss that and applaud short-term results because they cannot see that they are achieved at the expense of customer satisfaction. But they will not keep on applauding.

There is a ground swell from customers demanding service and they know when they are getting it. However, the bank stock analysts (and senior executives if they manage without much information except current figures) have difficulty determining the level of customer satisfaction and whether the future is looking better or worse. On the other hand, any unfavorable comparison with the previous year or quarter in the expense or profit figures pops right up. Managers must know and use today's figures, but also see beyond them or they risk crushing the attitudes and programs that have been successful and are most important for the future.

And we must work for the long-term benefit of all our constituencies, stockholders, customers, employees, and community, not just for a good rating by stock analysts. Bank stockholders have little chance of spectacular short-term profits. They do have every chance of benefitting over the years from sound programs."

49

Henry Ormsby

Senior Vice President
First National Bank of Louisville
Louisville, KY

Ronald G. Steinhart has put together a $4.7 billion banking organization with 49 offices in Texas since February 1988 by purchasing and successfully managing failed banks. He named his organization Team Bank because "so much of what we do we relates to the team spirit."

❝ Maybe 10 percent of the marketing ideas are great and 10 percent are bad. The others depend upon implementation. Coming up with a home run is not as important as putting together a good marketing program and making continuous and measurable progress over time.

❝If you can create a situation where everybody knows the company's objectives and all work together to achieve them, it's much better than everybody having their own agenda, no matter how good they are.

❝*The most important sale is to retain the current customers.* Our customer contact people

175

When an executive of a commercial borrower needs a loan for a lake house, it may need to be serviced in the bank's real estate department, but the customer should not have to prove himself all over again.

are trained to identify the customer's emerging needs and provide leads. Often those leads must be passed on to another department, which means teamwork, which is a big word with us.

"On a football team, the offensive tackle must make his block so the quarterback can throw a touchdown pass to the wide receiver. We must recognize the tackle's part. Our marketing plan depends on how we block and tackle.

"Everybody has a customer, either internal or external. Employees who are trying to serve the external customers cannot give (the customer) the best service possible, for example, from the operations center. In the long run your marketing effectiveness is tied directly to the effectiveness of your operational systems and day-to-day support.

The financial executive needs to understand figures and be able to tell whether they basically reflect the real situations; but mainly he needs to know what is behind the figures and the sound, profitable ways to improve them. That goes to a deep understanding of the whole industry, his organization, and its environment.

"In hiring customer contact people and management trainees, we put emphasis on sales orientation. While accounting is important, a liberal arts major with some accounting electives would certainly be looked on with favor in the trainee program."

Mr. Ormsby's bank is a $5 billion institution with a large number of branches all over that area. Having a good, solid marketing plan and "blocking and tackling" is behind all sales efforts. An outstanding banker salesman says, "Marketing is execution." If we do not execute do not blame the idea. There is an old military axiom that a fair plan understood and energetically executed beats a brilliant plan poorly carried out.

50

Richard Adams

Vice President and CEO
Bank of Commerce
Idaho Falls, ID

❝ We stick to 'the old basics' that used to be good years ago, like being good to our customers. Large banks move their bank people around and they don't have time to get acquainted. I hope they will never change that. People want to be known and called by name.

One executive said about bankers, **"They must not only be effective, they must be effective here."** A banker in one location may need a pin-striped suit, but one in another location may be better off with cowboy boots and a pickup.

"Our bank hires people who have grown up in this community. They have a following. We also like to hire people who have grown up on the farm, know how to work, and are quick to figure out and solve problems.

"We have 50,000 checking accounts which feed the rest of our business. We don't sponsor a credit card, but we do have a debit card, and

177

people know they have to have the money in the bank to be able to use it. In return, we don't have a service charge if they keep as much as $100 in their account.

There is no way to suitably emphasize the importance of quality. Good customers build and yield a profit. Bad ones cause loss. Get the good, and we will not reach for the bad.

"*Our big aim is to attract good customers.* Our officers teach about banking in the schools and how the young people should use their checking accounts. When these young people open an account here, we don't charge them anything until they get a job.

Strength will be even more vital if deposit insurance is modified.

"Our bank has just paid our 76th consecutive dividend, but we pay a modest dividend and build up our capital account. We are competing with large banks. By having a larger capital, we can make larger loans without participation, and this also makes our large depositors feel comfortable.

"We draw in quite a bit of deposits from beyond our area without having to pay an excessive rate, and I believe this is because of our strength. We are building a good, strong bank and letting people know about it.

"We have not had trouble with our agricultural loans. We would rather be conservative going in and not have so much trouble later. This is the reason we do not make 100 percent car loans, although our competitors do.

To stay out of the courthouse, banks can settle disagreements early. If the bank is wrong, admit it and pay. Have experienced people in sensitive positions. Keep good records on transactions that may cause disagreement.

"We don't like to go to court. I think it's a bad thing to read a bank's name in the paper in connection with a lawsuit.

"We have ten offices located within a 60 mile radius. There are 175,000 people in our county, and we generally go into small com-

Let us figure out how to please and make money on the good, small customer instead of letting him drift away. Many of the young people we ignore today will be important leaders tomorrow. Wrigley built a great business on a 5¢ package of chewing gum. Of course it costs more now, but it still retains its following.

munities with very few banks. This has been good to us."

*A*ttracting good customers. It is the customer who makes the bank. Good customers do not cause loan or overdraft problems. Their business grows so the bank will grow automatically. And 50,000 accounts to feed the business from now on! Banks that have discouraged good small customers to improve short-term profit will want them back later when they have grown—but will not be able to get them.

51

Judy R. Loving

Chairman of the Board
The Bank of Yellville
Yellville, AR

Through the efforts of one of its directors, The Bank of Yellville has researched and published the history of the bank and of the community, including how Yellville got its name. Tying the bank to the history and growth of the community adds a sense of strength and belonging. Customers will be less likely to go to a bank that they see as not a part of their history.

" The Bank of Yellville presents its customers with an annual calendar decorated with student art from the elementary and high schools of this north central Arkansas county. While most banks give their customers calendars, the beauty of our program is that we take dollars allocated to an existing marketing project and place them in a similar program that triples media exposure.

" Numerous opportunities for promotion—photographs, feature articles, radio interviews, and individual school activities—result naturally from the community's appreciation of the yearlong project. The student contest in spring and the announcement of winners in Septem-

ber are a prelude to the fanfare of the introduction of the calendar in late November.

"Our calendar project enables students to
publish their work, a fine experience for young
people. Parents obviously love it, as do grand-
parents and relatives across the country. Art
teachers are especially pleased, and principals
cannot say enough good things about the bank
for promoting their schools and young artists.

**These pictures
reflect real local
interests. The Bull
Shoals area has
experienced a
great resurgence
of wildlife
including bald
eagles, turkeys,
deer, and even
bears. Many other
institutions have
gained favorable
recognition by
focusing on local
scenes and
architecture.**

"The 8½ × 11 inch pages of the spiralbound
calendar are designed so that each month features an original drawing. The calendar pad
displays an apt quotation for the month, together with a note about specific banking
services relating to the central theme of the
season. For example, on the March page the
reader finds a pen-and-ink of a Canadian goose
in a natural marsh setting, sketched by Tracy
Burleigh of Yellville-Summit High School, a
quotation by William Wordsworth, and a note
about Individual Retirement Account invest-
ments. The rear cover contains a listing of the
bank's financial services, account opportunities, hours, and other information that a customer might need for handy reference.

"The calendar hangs in many homes and
businesses of the area as a daily reminder of
the community involvement and services provided by the Bank of Yellville. Additionally,
the project simultaneously promotes art in education and encourages the community's
young people, our future banking customers."

The Bank of Yellville is a $43 million bank
with offices in Yellville and Bull Shoals, Arkansas. It is the only locally owned community

bank in a five-county area. It was founded in 1946 by Mrs. Bernice Berry who managed it until her death in 1982. The bank is currently owned and operated in a very professional way by members of her family and others.

The Bank of Yellville emphasizes the role and training of directors and planning involving much of the staff. They also have attractive employees of high potential who take the extra steps that are so long remembered.

52

Bruce Roberts

President
Bank of Loleta
Eureka, CA

Many banks could use this idea, especially those with mountains, lakes, seashores, or vivid local history. Local public radio and television, historical societies, preservation and cultural groups, and the overwhelming popularity of the environmental movement are all activities in which the smart banker will be sincerely involved.

❝ Our best marketing idea has been to use a limited edition of prints of paintings of local scenes and historic landmarks. The artists are from our local group. It is important to the artist who has the opportunity to be reproduced in full color, and they sign numbered prints, generally from 500 to 1,000 for each painting.

❝ The bank offers to sell the package of prints for $50.00 to $75.00, or give it to customers who are establishing new relationships, for example, opening a checking account for more than $500. Generally the new accounts are many times that amount.

Time after time we see communities gain new life around local pride. Guthrie, Oklahoma, was just another old town until it made itself famous with its history as the place of the first great Oklahoma land run and the site of the original state capital. Stately old homes, some of which now offer bed and breakfast, remind people of days gone by. The banker who leads efforts to preserve such values will be rewarded by appreciation for his bank.

" At the opening of one of our banks, one print was of an architecturally and historically significant building and the other was one of our beautiful redwood forests. Generally the original hangs in the bank, but in one case, it was awarded in a drawing in connection with the opening.

" I often see these prints framed and hanging in homes and offices. Doing this in large numbers we are able to acquire the artwork very reasonably. The whole package costs us only about $2.50 to $3.00. *We have run this promotion three times and in each case it has added about $10 million to our deposits!*

" Our company is located in a fairly isolated area near the coast in Northern California. Our primary county has 105,000 people and we have an office also in the neighboring county, which borders on Oregon. We are second in market share only to Bank of America in this district."

Mr. Roberts came to the bank in 1976 when it was $15 million in total resources. It is now $165 million. Outstanding and creative management, with a strong focus on local interests, have contributed much to the bank's growth. The institution that is seen as an important part of community history takes on a strong aura of strength and authenticity.

The bank, of which I was CEO in East Dallas, started financing the restoration of old homes in the early '70s. Many had historic and architectural importance. I had underestimated the

powerful interest in these and other things of
unique local importance, such as trees planted
by the first settlers. Leadership by the bank in
such programs adds prestige as well as money
to the effort.

53

Jim Hill

Senior Vice President
Zion's First National Bank
Salt Lake City, UT

Finding out what customers (and others) really think of us is a courageous thing to do. How many of us would hear the same words as Jim Hill? How many are willing to?

❝ Interviews with customers who are leaving us show that they are not paying so much attention to price as we thought. *We found that if we give outstanding service and really understand the customer, we can charge.* Customers leaving wanted us to be more interested and concerned.

❝ A few years ago, I did a personal poll covering customers of our banks, other banks, business people, and, for example, a business editor of our local paper. I found they were using such words as 'arrogant, dull, uninteresting.' They were unimpressed with us as people.

"For the last two years, we have made some very impressive changes through training. We have ways of noticing little things that our employees are doing to provide outstanding service, and we have made some very important changes. Our cross-sell ratios are way up. We have been able to identify some heroes. We have also been able to identify people who really don't want to play this game. They have realized that they have limited career opportunities here.

"Our slogan for this year's training is, 'Everyone has a customer.' This means that people in the operations center have a customer, which is the loan officer, calling them for information so that he can service the customer. Our president talks to these people. He emphasizes that we can't give the kind of service necessary to make us the best bank in Salt Lake City unless they give the best kind of service to their customer, who is someone (officer or employee) in our bank calling them for help.

"**Everyone has a customer.**" This includes the controller, cashier, human resources, credit department, collectors, and, of course, the operations center, as well as all the people in direct contact with the customer. No financial institution, or medical clinic, or automobile agency, or any other business can give service of excellence until everyone understands and lives by that.

"*The difference between us and other banks is purely how well we execute these ideas.* It is a new world; competition is very keen. People don't have to plead with us to get a loan.

"When we go to the college campuses to recruit, we are looking not just for the bright young people, for those are heavy in accounting in finance, but for people who have shown sensititivity, humility, and interpersonal skills in general.

"But none of this works unless there is commitment right at the top. It is a new world."

Weldon Howell, one of the great creative bankers of Dallas, gave the illustration of a manager in his bank who did well "until he decided to become a heel." Many bankers got an exaggerated sense-of-self importance because of the power to lend other people's money.

"**H**umility" is a very important quality. Many bankers have thought they were important because they had the care of their neighbors money and could grant or deny loans. More humility would have brought many banks closer to the reason they were chartered—to serve the needs of their market areas.

Jim's bank is a part of a regional holding company with $3.5 billion in total assets, the second largest in the area. They are highly pleased with the progress that has resulted from this new emphasis, which includes job descriptions that help employees understand their part in achieving the bank's goals, including marketing objectives.

Job (responsibility) descriptions should be a natural result of banking strategy which includes departmental planning and objectives. These goals must be agreed on by the individuals in each department. The person occupying a specific position can expand the job description through ambition, ability, and experience. Put someone of greater ability, experience, and scope in any job, and it will immediately get bigger.

A supervisor can also help enrich the job. The job description should not limit the job, but be a basis for understanding it. It should outline major responsibilities and avoid details. In many areas (e.g. wire transfer, exchange department) specific procedures must be outlined and followed. Generally, they belong in a manual of procedure that is kept up-to-date. For example, tellers in most banks go through similar procedures. But one bank expects tellers to make a sales approach designed to get referrals from their contacts, another places premiums on speed and accuracy. These exemplify job responsibilities that vary with the objectives of the bank, the department, the boss, and the individual.

The job description should be worked out by the supervisor and the person doing the job. Both should be looking for ways to practice job enrichment.

54

Loan By Phone

This is such a big subject that I would like to present the ideas of diverse types of institutions from varying sections of the country.

A

Richard S. D'Agostino

Executive Vice President
Beneficial Banc
Philadelphia, PA

Loan-by-phone programs that expect to (generally) give an answer while the customer is on the telephone (first call usually) depend on having telephone answerers who are credit-wise and on technology that enables the person on the telephone to screen several credit bureaus simultaneously.

❝ A 'loan-by-telephone' program must be well supported by advertising. The public does become familiar with the fact that you have a loan-by-phone program, but when we advertise its productivity can be quadrupled. The advertising expense is insignificant compared to the volume and the profit that can be produced.

❝ We found that we produced more home equity loans and personal loans than auto loans. Perhaps there is something missing in the way we are presenting the auto loan.

❝ Any consumer loan must have three elements:

- The right price
- Correct servicing
- A delivery mechanism

"The loan by telephone, of course, is the delivery mechanism. Many finance companies have small closing offices, perhaps 400 square feet in an office building. Some companies even close loans at the borrower's home. We have not done that, but we are not ruling it out. Our telephone service operates 9 A.M. to 9 P.M. daily, Saturday from 9 A.M. to 5 P.M., and Sunday from noon to 5 P.M.

"All of the information given to us by the customer over the telephone has been confirmed before the loan is committed and, of course, in the face-to-face closing we get positive identification and check any other matters that might need attention at that time.

"Although there are more rejections among the loan-by-phone applicants, the quality of the loans that are originated by telephone is every bit as good as those originated in the branches.

"The people handling the telephone calls are credit experienced. They are tied directly into the credit bureaus and strive to give an approval before they get off the phone. All of this is subject to verification. The loans are actually closed in the branches where we do the cross-selling.

"Where loans are complex we steer the customer to a branch."

B

Karen Davis

Vice President of Marketing
USAA Federal Savings Bank
San Antonio, TX

▌▌ To get a loan, a member (a member of the armed services or a dependent) would call in on a toll-free number, talk to someone in the National Sales and Service Division who probably has available a credit limit. Technology enables you to simultaneously screen several credit bureaus as determined by the application which you are receiving over the telephone. If the loan is fairly simple (for instance, a car loan), the member might get the loan commitment on the initial call. In any event, you would expect to give an answer that day. Giving service is your number one priority. From the point of committing the auto loan, for example, to completion of the transaction, it would be as if the member had called a local bank with which he did business.

"A member overseas who is returning to the United States might call, for example, and arrange an auto loan so that the car could be waiting for him on the dock in San Francisco or wherever he comes in. If he has selected a home and wishes the purchase, the home loan can be already in place before he returns from overseas."

Loan by phone has been rejected by some because of the cost of advertising or because it is thought difficult to cultivate a strong customer relationship. Yet, it is not so different from the mass loan production engaged in by many banks (including our own) that financed appliances years ago. In this day of jammed highways and slow mail delivery, loan by phone has a lot to recommend it for customer convenience.

55

Robert Dye

Vice President and Director of Marketing
Gary-Wheaton Bank
Wheaton, IL

One of the country's most all around experienced bank marketers is Bob Dye, Vice President and Director of Marketing of Gary-Wheaton Banks, Wheaton, IL, a six bank holding company in the Chicago area.

Bob says, "The first job in developing a good marketing program, is to identify and remove the barriers or roadblocks that stand in the way of the full use of our resources to produce more profitable sales. Don't spend a penny on marketing until this has been done."

PART THREE

Removing The Barriers To Good Marketing

Find the barriers to good marketing in your bank and get them down. Bob Dye (idea 55) says, "We must lower the barriers between our major marketing resources and our objective of making more and more profitable sales. Do this before you spend a penny on marketing." There are many possible barriers that can prevent your employees from achieving profitable sales, as illustrated below:

```
┌─────────────────────┐
│     RESOURCES       │
└─────────────────────┘
```

Directors
Employees
Capital

Customer
Product
Facilities
Service
Image
Others

**COMMON ROADBLOCKS
BETWEEN RESOURCES AND SALES**

Lack of Management Interest
Undefined Market Focus
Poor Hiring Practices
Low Morale/Bad Attitude
Lack of Training
High Turnover
Not Knowing Customers or Products
No Help From Directors and Stockholders
Bad Reputation in Community
Ineffective Organization for Marketing
Poor Service
Lack of Leadership
Poor Communication
And Many Others

SALES

A common barrier to good marketing may be
the lack of a clear idea of what markets we do
and do not want to serve. One of the reasons
for marked differences in performance has
been due to the banks' definition of its market.
This is especially true in lending. In many
cases, banks to not even have a formal definition. In the old days, banks felt responsible to

serve all the financial needs of their geographical community. A bank may still want to do that (especially in smaller towns where it takes all the local business to support a bank, and the bank generally has knowledge of most customers), but the responsibility is not the same—anybody can come into that market. The Merrill Lynch 800 number reaches the smallest hamlet. Banks, in turn, have the right to decide what may be their most promising and profitable sectors of the market, while being careful to avoid dangerous concentration of credit.

The market definition should be carefully made. Avoid what one banker calls "the new religion." Some banker (probably far down in the organization) may hear that nobody is making commercial loans under $500,000 or $1,000,000 and takes this as gospel. Hearsay should not be the basis for policy formulation.

Barriers to successful bank selling include lack of interest and cooperation on the part of officers and employees. Expressions formerly used, like, "Marketing is not my job," or "The man who writes the advertising does not make the loans," reflect attitudes banks can no longer afford. We are competing with organizations and people who have lived by selling. Salespeople in the brokerage business who survived bad years still found ways to make commissions. Retailers learned to stand on their feet and sell from 10:00 in the morning to 10:00 at night during the Christmas rush. These people are now our competitors. They do not have to be taught how to sell. We do. Thus, lack of sales training is another barrier and is a part of management's responsibility.

Banks are also competing with the other financial institutions that are good at marketing and offer outstanding products and service from bottom to top. They are as ready to gobble up business of the inept marketers as any other competitor. Remember, though, while most salespeople can simply be out there selling, the banker must be an effective salesperson with his guard up. Bankers do not want to open an account or make a loan to just anybody. Selling financial service requires both judgement and sales expertise.

Another common barrier is lack of general *training*. Poorly trained employees cost business and cause expensive mistakes, including lawsuits. While many banks have reduced or eliminated training because of a profit squeeze, others are emphasizing it. Some are spending amounts on training that would have been thought extreme a few years ago. Who is right? The profit proof and the survival proof (over a period of time) are that the trainers are right *if* the job is done well and tied to total customer service and good management.

Part of training should include how to deal with an angry customer—the importance of what one banker called "losing a customer as gracefully as we gain one." Inexperienced bankers must be taught that when we cannot satisfy a customer we must be sure they go out knowing we tried.

As Lowell Smith, Jr., Chairman of the First State Bank of Rio Vista, Texas, said, "Bankers must admit the bank's mistakes and correct them quickly and pleasantly." This is especially true of those errors that might lead to lawsuits. Banks lose much when they come

head-to-head with their customers in court or
out. The banker must be able to avoid bad
feelings and really communicate with the customers. If the customer understands there is a
sensible reason for the bank's action, many ir-
ritations will disappear. Directors and spouses
can play a big part as ambassadors in the community.

Few bank employees want to do a poor job, but
they must know how to do a good one. We
need to provide training before customer contact is made. When employees do not know
how to do the job, they often become defen-
sive, rather than simply admitting they do not
know and asking for the customer's cooperation.

In preparing a seminar on communication I
asked several bankers for examples of poor
communication in their banks and what they
cost. They were legion—and that is not just in
banking. The head of a large utility gave me
similar examples. This may be a reflection of
education's reduced emphasis on communication; businesses and individuals are on their
own.

Through proper training, banks can minimize
mistakes and soften their effects. As a busi-
nessman, I borrow money from banks, and we
often transfer funds. Most of the bank contact
is between my assistant and bank operations
people. We had to move significant business
away from a bank for which I had a strong
affection because we could not afford to spend
so much of our time correcting bank mistakes.
Some institutions are paying the customer if
the bank makes a mistake, or if a customer
waits in line more than five minutes or suffers

or receives other poor service. Good idea, but training can reduce the need for such measures.

One banker, asked for his best marketing idea, said, "blocking and tackling." This means going back to basics: calling on our customers as well as the prospects; doing a good job in writing letters and on the telephone; wearing proper attire; calling the customer by name and providing good, personal service; being accurate, correcting mistakes quickly and in good spirits; and, in general, as one banker put it, "doing most things that were good for banks in the past."

Employees must know what products the bank has to sell, who does it, and who needs it. Recently, I went to a large department store trying to buy a work shirt and some gloves with wrist protection which I could use to work in my garden infected with poison ivy. This was a beautiful new store with acres of merchandise and eager salespeople, but nobody knew what was in the store or where it was. How many savings products did your bank have a few years ago? And how many do you have today? Do your people know what is in the store and who provides it?

If we had to calculate the real cost of turnover and look at it, we would pay more attention. One banker estimates it costs $50,000 to replace a loan officer. This includes lost contacts and business and a lower collection record on his difficult loans.

Turnover is another barrier. In many banks, turnover is a chief cause of the loss of business, lost contact, and reduced likelihood of collecting troublesome loans. It also raises salary costs by forcing the bank to pay more for a good replacement. A customer complains that his bank gives him a new loan officer on the average of every nine months. This is common. These new officers may be good people, but the customer has a great sense of insecurity when introduced to one new banker after another. The relationship is weakened and the customer is open to approach from others. At the least, he may seek another connection as a back up. What do we hear around many banks—exluding the country banks? "I do not know anybody there anymore." For an alert competitor, that spells opportunity. But can we really promise that they will know anybody at our place after a few months?

We have identified many possible barriers to effective marketing. *Every bank should make its own inventory.* One of the most deadly is lack of real interest by employees, management, and supervisors. Asking our customers and employees to identify our faults is a great help. Do not fail to check telephone communication. How hard is it to get your people on the telephone? If officers are not available, does someone make more of an effort than to say, "He is in a meeting." How many calls are unreturned at the end of the day? How many letters sound cold and remote? There should be an occasional look at everything that is going out of the bank and what impression it makes.

The *attitude* that a bank portrays plays an important role in creating or overcoming barriers. I was doing some work in a $30 million independent bank and happened to overhear a conversation in the bookkeeping department with a customer who had called about an account. Believe it or not, the bank employee said essentially, "I do not have time to talk about this now. Call me back in two or three days." The CEO was sitting in his office scrambling to build business and overcome problems. He did not know that was happening. No institution can treat the customer like that and meet the effective and ever-increasing competition from financial institutions that are really outstanding in customer relations. There are more of them all the time.

Negative attitudes of the board of directors sometimes constitute a strong barrier to effective selling. I once had a director who told people in the community I was going to break the bank. If a director did that now, he or she would be believed. Such a director should get a little woodshed conversation from the chairman or other directors. An earlier, and more gentle step, is the development of a code of director conduct. This does not mean everything is milk and honey, but it does mean some straight talk.

Bad community image can also be a powerful and hard force to fight. At a recent roundtable of 12 bank CEOs in Texas, it was noted that customers today are very concerned with the soundness of financial institutions. When customers lose confidence, they just fade away. "How can we restore faith in our strength and integrity?" is a question most bankers never thought they would have to ask. "Do a good job, demonstrate performance, get directors and spouses to be good ambassadors, be sure officers and employees believe in what the bank is doing and actually use our services themselves," were some of the suggestions. "Sell total reliability."

In working on some recent books, I had interviews with many CEOs and directors. On rare occasions I asked them where they carried on their personal banking, and the answers were sometimes surprising. If they were not using their own bank, there may be an understandable reason. For example, the CEO should not borrow from his own shop, for, in my view, who can say "no" to him? Others disagree. The bank may not be big enough for the director's borrowings, and the director may feel like a captive. It is possible, though, that a great number of our people bank somewhere else because they like it better. If banks cannot sell their own people, they had better take notice.

A vital step in developing a cost-effective marketing program is for management to get everyone involved. This especially includes the board of directors, and for the independent bank, the stockholders. Involvement should include every part of the team—even those who clean the bank at night and provide security. Everybody on the team should know the bank's goals. For example, in developing its profit plan, one bank set out a goal to add $25 million net in loans outstanding, all under proper safeguards. At the time the plan was developed, one of the major lending departments was actually trying to reduce loans. They were not doing it under that banner, nor was it out of conservatism. They were still operating with last year's attitudes. Up-to-date objectives of the bank need to be communicated, and divided to departments, and by the departments to individuals, and then everyone must understand what the objectives are and the role they play in reaching them. Peters and Waterman, in their book, *Search for Excellence*, note that the employee cannot take us where we are going unless they know where that is. Not profound, but powerful.

In this way, the whole bank becomes a sales force, with each member contributing in his

own way—through direct selling, or providing
service, or simply doing the primary job in a
way that contributes to the whole. Gone is the
skepticism with which prospects brought in by
other officers or employees are greeted by the
lenders; gone is the attitude of the loan officer
that says the ball is always in the borrower's
court; gone is the belated response, "Oh, didn't
we give you an answer?" There is no excuse for
the employee to show the customer the attitude, "I just do not have time for you," even if
the bank is thin on staff.

The ability to get sound loans with good yields
and reasonable liquidity and without a concentration of credit is, and will be, the measure of
the growth and prosperity of most banks. This
is not to advocate lowering credit quality. Risks
can best be reduced by good loan officers with
an outstanding supporting cast getting and
keeping good customers. *It is safer to seek
loans that meet the bank's criteria than to wait
for whatever walks in.* If a customer has credit
lines at two banks (as many do), he will soon
find he is doing most of the business with the
one he feels best about.

Many banks neglect to use their lobby space
for selling. Thus, large percentages of our customers remain unfamiliar with all the services
offered. Does your bank make residential real
estate loans? What percentage of your customers know?

The old attractive signs advertising home improvement loans or even available lock boxes
have disappeared from most lobbies. When
bank products are proliferating, many banks
are keeping that a secret. Oh, we have publications in a rack, but who is going to read them?
No wonder a banker who opened a branch in a

supermarket found that the store's displays were more attractive than those of the bank.

When a bank is really ready to emphasize marketing, it should develop a program by looking first at the most promising opportunities in which the bank already has a foothold. One banker says, "If banks would ever consolidate their business, they would never need to run another ad." He emphasizes the importance of a new accounts department as a center for getting additional business from every new account customer. He advocates that every new customer should meet a loan officer and two tellers. Also, many of our customers are making note payments with checks on other banks and showing on their financial statements deposit balances and loans with other institutions. There are so many of these opportunities that we tend to be dismayed by their sheer magnitude. The reason banks do a poor job of following the internally generated leads is that there are so many of them. Some banks have a carefully developed system that includes follow-up; they usually get great results for little cost. If you cannot do a thorough job now, pick an area and start.

Some banks are already well-organized. Tellers are expected to develop a percentage of leads, and if above that, they make incentive pay. The same policy could work out of the credit department, or note payment window, or many other places. Those receiving referrals could get paid for appointments made or customers secured. Payments should not be so great, though, as to overweigh discretion.

Most banks assign the responsibility for knowing and contacting a present customer to one officer or employee; some even have a backup.

But there must be an occasional verification that we actually *are* making contact with these customers. In all these efforts management should follow and supervise, otherwise we do not mean it.

To be effective in supervising the marketing effort, the CEO and other executives must know more than the figures on the printout. They need to get into the banks, the departments, and the customer's places of business; they need to know what is going on.

Related to this issue are comments made to me by three executives:

1. Alice De Souza, Senior Vice President, Bank of New Hampshire Corporation. "A marketing person or chief financial officer who thinks he can succeed in the future without knowing how the bank makes its money, will not be successful." Marketing in banking, as elsewhere, must be seen as a profit maker.

2. Willaim M. Fackler, Executive Vice President, Barnett Banks, Inc. "Our marketing program is more a function of how the local president manages and uses the individual market flavor to gain the competitive advantage."

The CEO has to be in there pitching and leading, and the whole effort *must fit this market*, not some other.

3. Ronald G. Steinhart, Chairman and CEO, Team Bank, Dallas. "The only way we can be more successful than others is to be better marketers."

Keep Looking For Great Ideas

When asked for his best marketing idea, one fine CEO said, "Keep your eyes open and steal all the good ideas you can." Opportunities abound, especially at conventions and seminars. "What are you doing in your bank that is working well?" creates an opening. Outstanding bankers adopt many great ideas from outside banking.

During combat in Germany in World War II, I saw signs that said something like "5,482 miles to Wall Drug." "What in the world is Wall Drug?" I thought. I did not realize then that such signs were all over the world, even Antartica. Wall Drug is advertised on London's double-decker buses, and this organization is often used as a case study in business schools. Last summer we were in Wall, South Dakota, on the edge of the Badlands. It is a town that would not even be there if it were not for Wall Drug, which attracts 1.5 million customers annually. A young couple started it at the bottom of the depression in 1931, partly because they wanted to be in a community where they could attend Mass everyday. Five years later they were about to give up.

On a particularly hot Sunday afternoon Dorothy Husted, the wife in this entrepreneurial couple, was trying to take a nap with the children but was interrupted by the noise of the jalopies on a nearby highway. The husband said he was sorry. The wife said, "Don't be, because it has given me an idea. What do these people want after this long drive across a barren stretch? Ice water. (No auto air-conditioning then.) We have plenty of water and plenty of ice. Let us advertise free ice water." The husband said he felt rather foolish out there, putting up on the highway Burma Shave type signs that ended with "Free ice water." But, by the time he got back to the store, there were already people in there asking for the ice water and buying other things as well. Now they sell a vast array of merchandise in a business that covers more than a square block, and they still provide a good cup of coffee for 5¢.

Wall Drug made an unbelievable success out of near failure through finding what the customer wanted and giving it to him. In the financial field there are many ideas about selling the customer what we want him to have—that it is an uphill battle. Ted Husted says of Wall Drug, "What you need to do is reach out to people with something they need."

There is also the remarkable story of L. L. Bean, the great merchandiser of outdoor–type clothing and equipment in the little town of Freeport, Maine. "L. L." started his now famous business as a part of a shoe store when he developed the Maine Hunting Boot. Now the store sends over 100 million catalogues and in 1988 had more than 3.5 million customers visit the retail location. A whole community has been built around them. The story of L. L. Bean has been said to be one of selling total reliability and complete customer satisfaction.

There are some similar spectacular possibilities in banking. Just consider the Rio Vista State Bank in Texas, over $127 million bank in a town of 460 people! And it is a strong, highly profitable institution run by rock solid bankers. In our marketing programs, let us not give so much attention to internals that we forget to find out what the customer wants.

Hank Wyatt, long-time, highly respected Texas banker, said, "Your best marketing program is to take care of your customers one at a time, and remember, one of the biggest marketing tools is referrals." The referrals come from happy customers who have been served "one customer at a time."

In all things the leader must lead. The CEO who preaches customer service and holding down expenses will not be listened to if he parks the bank-owned luxury car in the most convenient parking space that should be reserved for customers.

Ed Eastham, president of a bank in Fort Worth, said, "I tried to get my officers to talk to customers in the lobby. I finally decided I needed to lead by example. Now I spend some time every day . . . out in the lobby, and the officers are willing to follow suit."

Areas in which the leader must take charge are in defining the market, studying the market, and keeping up with what is happening in the market. A wrong market definition can lead to disaster. In Dallas, in the early 80s, many lenders thought they were dealing with a real estate market that would always go up. Inflation had covered most of the mistakes we made earlier as real estate lenders. But when there were fewer rich people to buy luxury properties, that market crumbled. When the oil service companies began going out of business in the early 80s they no longer needed office space. Many lenders could have been more closely attuned to what was happening in the market, especially those from far away (who should probably not have been in such a distant market at all). Sale prices of single family residences in some Texas cities fell 40 percent or more, so even private mortgage insurance would not make the bank whole. Now, declines are occurring in other parts of the country. What is happening in your market? That is always a critical question.

Studying the market must be constant. Use all the tools, all the time, and get input. One executive committee chairman said, "I drive a different route everyday." In this way, he gets to view various alternatives and options. The spouses of our officers and directors and employees are often the most neglected tool in banking. Ask for their help; let them know what we are doing and why.

The most lasting impressions on customers are those actions that go beyond anything that might have been expected.

As a part of my consulting business, I have worked with many outstanding law firms. One of these is Shartsis, Freise, and Ginsburg in San Francisco. Returning from lunch with two of their attorneys, I had an attack of vertigo (which has been a problem for years). It can make you very sick, but not seriously. These attorneys summoned the ambulance; one accompanied me to the emergency room, called my secretary, and put my doctor in touch with the emergency room physician. The lead secretary asked her doctor to assist and two members of the firm left me their home numbers! This is going way beyond the call of duty and makes a lasting impression.

Most bankers have had many opportunities of this kind and their customers have said, "I never will forget when you helped me with. . . ." We can seize many of these opportunities with little cost and earn the loyalty of worthwhile customers.

One of the best features of our business is that, properly served, the good customer tends to stay, to recommend us to others, and to buy more services from us all the time if they are pleased. What more could we ask of any business?

Index